JONATHAN MAITLAND

metro

Published by Metro Publishing Ltd,
3, Bramber Court, 2 Bramber Road,
London W14 9PB, England

www.blake.co.uk

First published in hardback in 2005

ISBN 1 84358 143 4

British Library Cataloguing-in-Publication Data:

A catalogue record for this book is available from the British Library.

Design by www.envydesign.co.uk

Printed in Great Britain by Creative Print & Design (Wales)

1 3 5 7 9 10 8 6 4 2

Papers used by Metro Publishing are natural, recyclable products made from
wood grown in sustainable forests. The manufacturing processes conform to
the environmental regulations of the country of origin.

Cartoons by Anthony Kelly
kellyscartoons@btinternet.com
www.cartoonists.co.uk/kelly

For Emily,
who gets my vote,
every time

CONTENTS

PROLOGUE

On the morning of 22 May 2004, a rectangular brown envelope shuffled through my letter box. Once upon a time it might have contained something pleasant, like a party invite or a love letter. This, I suspected, was neither – mainly because it had a red logo thing stamped on the front which read, 'Hammersmith and Fulham Council: Serving our Community'. Arse, I thought. We only moved in two weeks ago and they're already asking us for money.

It was a council tax demand. For a lot of wonga: £2,262.80. More than £40 a week. I've never been asked to pay that much in my life. I spent the day ranting – at my wife, the guy on the next exercise bike at the gym and Graham, the bloke who sells newspapers outside Stamford Brook tube station. 'Two thousand pounds. TWO THOUSAND POUNDS! For what, exactly? What do we get in return?' That kind of thing.

No one had any satisfactory answers. But there was a

lot of shrugging and, 'Yeah, know what you mean, terrible isn't it?' stuff going on. Which got me thinking. I should have known the answers myself. But I didn't. I didn't have a clue about the council tax. Or the council. In fact, I was shockingly ignorant about politics, full stop: a political dunce. Despite being a law graduate, a reporter on the most popular current affairs programme on TV and 43 years old, I knew as much about politics as I did about what lies beneath a car bonnet. I knew what it was there for, but had absolutely no idea how all the different bits and pieces fitted together.

Until recently this hadn't bothered me. Whenever I'd been given a political story, I used to get by – just – using a combination of front, common sense and other people. Anyway, there were more interesting things to do, like cricket, Scrabble and eating sausages.

But then, like a lot of other people, when we invaded Iraq I got what they call 'politicised'... a bit. I started asking questions such as, 'How can this be happening when so many people are dead against it?' and – a big one, this – 'Er... What's democracy all about, anyway?'

I realised there were a lot of people like me – reasonably intelligent, moderately civic-minded types who had the same Grand Canyon-sized gaps in their knowledge. It's no use reading the papers or watching TV: they're not big on explaining political stuff in a cut out-and-keep/let's-start-from-the-beginning kind of way. They don't explain, for instance, how one party can get more votes than the other but still lose the election.

Or what they mean by, 'The Bill has reached the committee stage in the House of Commons.' And European Health and Safety Directives. What are they? Where do they come from, exactly? And do they really mean my local butcher's pork-and-apple sausages are going to be banned?

I realised I knew the answer to none of the above. So I decided to find out. Which is why I am writing this book. I'm not trying to educate everyone to PhD standard; I'm just hoping you'll know more useful stuff at the end than you did at the beginning. And with luck, it might help you hold your own at parties when the chat turns vaguely political. I don't have an agenda, either: I'm trying to tell it like it is. This isn't one of those books that puts two and two together and comes up with five. If you want conspiracy theories – as in 'President Bush knew about 9/11 in advance, you know' – you've come to the wrong place. The aim here is to try and find out a bit more about the way our country works. I don't mean to be pompous, but that brown envelope from the council didn't just change my bank balance: it also, in a small but significant way, changed my life. I want to find out more. Lots more. Are you sitting comfortably? Then let us begin!

CHAPTER ONE

Let us Pay: Where do our Taxes go?

I drive a ludicrous car. But I don't care. It's an electric-blue, second-hand Nissan Micra and I bought it last year. I once read that Nissan Micras were the most repellent cars on the road. I can see why. Mine is particularly revolting. It has vomit-like patterns etched into the paintwork and looks like a hairdryer on wheels. But I love it because it's cheap to run, gets me from A to B and I can always find a parking space.

The Nissan cost me £2,500. Which, by unhappy coincidence, is only slightly more than my annual council tax bill. But that's where the similarity ends. With my car, I can see exactly what my money's brought me, every day of the week: four tyres, an engine and a steering wheel. And some stuff under the bonnet I don't understand. The benefits from my council tax aren't so apparent. Not to me, anyway. And I'm not alone. I asked my mate Mark, who used to work in the City, what his was for. Like me, he knew it helped provide local services, but he wasn't sure which. He thought it might have something to do with bins.

I'm not the only one who hates paying tax. Most of us do, obviously. But then we always have. The ancient Greeks complained about it. Lady Godiva got her kit off because there was so much of it. And The Beatles wrote a protest song, 'Taxman', about it, in which George Harrison listed an impressive number of things the Taxman had his eyes on. One item George didn't mention, however, was windows. In 1696 they started to tax them at sixpence a time. Even now, if you look

hard enough, you can still see buildings with windows that have been bricked in: an early form of tax avoidance. No wonder they waited 250 years before inventing double glazing.

If you had a window-friendly house that was also full of dogs, then you were really in trouble. That's because 17th-century British pooches were also taxed. The assessor used to go round houses at night kicking doors and charging home owners according to the amount of barking he could hear.

No history of taxation, however brief, would be complete without mentioning the French connection. They are the reason we pay income tax. When Napoleon started misbehaving, we went to war with him. It was very expensive. So income tax was introduced by Prime Minister William Pitt in 1799, to help feed and arm the troops. Yet another thing to blame the French for, then.

The big problem with tax is that it's hard to see what we get in return, compared to other stuff we spend money on, such as my Nissan Micra. That's one of the reasons why we complain about it so much. But governments *expect* that level of resentment: they build it into the system. The aim is to charge as much as possible, without causing a popular uprising. Or, as Louis XVI's finance minister Jean-Baptiste Colbert put it, the art of taxation is to 'Pluck the maximum amount of feathers from the goose with the least amount of hissing.'

When I read that quote it made me think. 'Hello,' I said to myself. 'Time to hiss a bit.'

I asked the Director of Finance at my local council, Hammersmith and Fulham, for an interview. I wanted her to explain to me and you how our money is spent. She refused. Her reasons, conveyed to me via a press officer, were that she didn't like talking to the media. That pissed me off a bit. I'm only trying to make people more aware of what's going on with our money, after all. And what's more, our money pays her wages. In fact we, the public, pay the salaries of every single director of finance in every single local authority in the country. So it wasn't unreasonable, I thought, to ask one of them to enlighten me. I sent her an email – see the next page.

Then I remembered that I had lived in another borough – Wandsworth – for 13 years, and that they might be more obliging. They were. A few days later I met Simon Heywood, Wandsworth Council's Director of Finance. He's also Deputy Chief Executive.

Mr Heywood is tall, in his 50s, bald and wears glasses. I couldn't help noticing his eyebrows: monstrously hairy ridges. Each could support the weight of a 50p piece. Simon's wages come in at a lot more, however: he earns 160 grand a year.

'Er... that's a lot of money. How can you justify being paid that much?'

Silence. Buttock shift. (Mine, not his.) Smile.

'Oh... I don't think I want to justify how much I get paid, actually. It's not down to me... it's the council's decision.'

Sorry to bother you

From: Jonathan Maitland
Sent: 16 August 2004 11:41
To: Jane West
Subject: Sorry to bother you

Dear Jane West

I'm just writing to thank you for giving me such a useful insight into how you and your council operate.
At first, when you let it be known that you didn't want to be interviewed for the book I am writing about politics, I was miffed. But then I thought about it. If you, who's paid by us to spend huge amounts of our money, don't think it's important to explain where it goes, then you have shown - far more revealingly than any interview - the council's attitude to us and our money.
I'm assuming you still can't spare the time, so could you please just email me the answers to the following questions:
1. How much of our money does the local council get every year?
2. How much do we pay you, personally, to spend it?
3. Any chance of a refund? Our bins haven't been emptied for weeks.
Cheers!

Jonathan Maitland

Fair enough. I just wanted to see if he'd tell me. Interestingly, he gets around forty grand a year more than the British Prime Minister. Is he on too much, or is the PM being paid too little?

Next question.

'I hate paying council tax… why do we have it at all? Can't we just abolish it?'

Mr Heywood looked slightly pained at my stupidity. He was very polite, though. He told me that if we didn't have it, the government would still need to raise the same amount, using another tax. If it didn't exist, in other words, we'd have to invent it.

OK. Next up. He gets £600 million of public money a year to keep the London Borough of Wandsworth – population 275,000 – alive and kicking. How does he spend it?

'Ooh, on lots of things.'

Who ate all the pie charts? I did. Mr Heywood gave them to me for lunch. His figures were for Wandsworth, obviously, but they could be applied to any council in the country. So this, ladies and gentlemen, is what your council tax goes towards:

1. Education. By far the biggest expense for any local council. Wandsworth pours almost 30 per cent of the housekeeping money into running the borough's schools.

2. Social services – old people's homes, meals on wheels, day-care centres, children's homes, paying for social workers to keep an eye on kids with dodgy parents, etc. This is nearly always the second most expensive item on any council shopping list.

7

3. Housing. Your council, like Wandsworth's, spends a few million a year running, cleaning and decorating local-authority-owned houses and flats. Yes, the council receives rent for these properties. But not enough to cover its costs.

4. The environment. Parks and commons need to be maintained; bins need emptying; streets need cleaning. I am beginning to hate the council tax a bit less.

5. Culture. Local theatres are given free money – grants – to stage shows. In Wandsworth, the Battersea Arts Centre is one such beneficiary. (This once, I recall, enabled them to put on a play performed entirely in Polish.)

6. Planning. Councils need departments that say 'yes' or 'no' to people wanting to build anything from garden sheds to shopping centres to noisy, smelly waste-recycling plants.

7. Highways – ie road maintenance. Yes, we are talking about one of the Great Political Issues of the 20th century. Potholes. Again, Wandsworth – like most councils – makes money out of its roads from things such as parking fines and parking permits. Hence those bloodthirsty traffic wardens who prowl the borough's pavements day and night, sometimes in packs of six. But overall, the money earned from all these activities isn't significant, despite appearances to the contrary.

8. Police and fire services. Our council tax pays their wages. In London this stuff is actually looked after by the Greater London Authority (GLA) – if you look closely at your council tax bill you will see what proportion of it goes to the GLA. If you don't live in London, I apologise. I know there's more to Britain than just London. If you are one of those chip-on-the-shoulder northern types, hate me.

I don't want to go into too much detail here: the phrase 'local government accounting' is a bit of a conversation stopper. And this book is supposed to be a thumbnail sketch, not a master class. But let us pause for a moment, as something curious is at play here. Our council tax payments, on their own, don't remotely cover the costs of all the above services. No way. In Wandsworth, for example, Simon Heywood apparently needs £600 million a year: but only £70 million of that comes directly from the pockets of local residents.

The rest comes mainly from a massive central government bucket, and is doled out by the Treasury. These hand-outs are called 'specific government grants', or 'formula grants'. This central government bucket is filled to the brim with billions of pounds raised from all the other taxes we pay – income tax, VAT and all those so-called stealth taxes we keep hearing about, such as the ones on booze, fags, petrol and roads.

Hold on a minute. This is a bit strange. We pay loads

of money to the government in taxes – and they then *pay it back* to our local councils. Our money travels halfway round the country, only for it to end up back where it started. Not very efficient, is it? Wouldn't it be more sensible to cut out the middle man – ie the government – and let us pay our local councils directly?

It might be. But there's a reason for the present system: control. In the UK, central government bods like to keep a close eye on local government bods. They don't want them to have too much leeway, as they might do something bonkers, like blow the entire social services budget on street parties. The most effective way for central government to keep control is via the purse strings. Which is why we have this round-the-houses payments system. Crucially, the system also lets the central government lot do their Robin Hood bit: 'reallocate' money from richer areas to poorer ones. It's called spreading the jam more evenly. This whole weird local/national finance thing is important, though, as it symbolises a Big Political Question. Which is: 'How do we want to be governed – locally, or nationally?' (Try lobbing that in to the dinner-party chat between main course and dessert.)

At the moment, central government holds the whip hand. But in Sweden, for example, it's the opposite: their local councils are mini kingdoms. That's because Swedes believe power should flow from the bottom up (no jokes, please). Hence the massively high rate of council tax over there. In fact, Swedish local authorities get around 80 per cent of their dosh *directly* from local

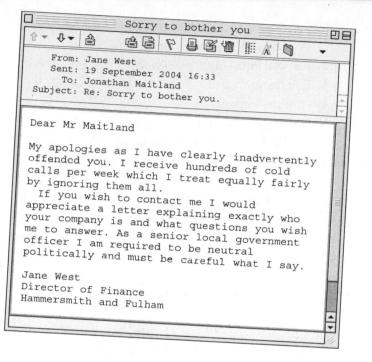

Sorry to bother you

From: Jane West
Sent: 19 September 2004 16:33
To: Jonathan Maitland
Subject: Re: Sorry to bother you.

Dear Mr Maitland

My apologies as I have clearly inadvertently offended you. I receive hundreds of cold calls per week which I treat equally fairly by ignoring them all.

If you wish to contact me I would appreciate a letter explaining exactly who your company is and what questions you wish me to answer. As a senior local government officer I am required to be neutral politically and must be careful what I say.

Jane West
Director of Finance
Hammersmith and Fulham

people. So, next time someone trots out those tired old clichés about Sweden (Abba, Volvo etc.), you could try giving them something new to think about.

OK, I've covered the ways that our money is spent locally, but what about nationally? How does all that income tax, VAT and national insurance get carved up? Well, in 2003, the government spent £419 billion. It shelled out, on average, more than £7,000 on behalf of every man, woman and child in the UK. The majority of that money – 70 per cent of it – went on the following :

1. Social security – ie dole money, pensions and all the various benefits on offer
2. The National Health Service
3. Education
4. Law and order
5. Defence
6. Transport

Sorry to bother you

From: Jonathan Maitland
Sent: 20 September 2004 11:25
To: Jane West
Subject: Re: Sorry to bother you

Dear Jane West

I appreciate and accept your apology, thank you. And as I said before, your refusal was more helpful and revealing than any interview could have been. I did actually list the exact questions I wanted to ask you, by the way, but not to worry: I've got the answers now.

Mind you, your email made me think. So I do have one more question: how would you feel if you spent £2,500 on a car, and were then told by the company that had taken your money, that their customer service policy was to treat all enquiries: 'equally fairly by ignoring them all'?

Just wondering, that's all…

Jonathan Maitland

Which of the above costs us the most, do you think? Health? Wrong. Education? Wrong again. It's social security. Almost a third of ALL the money the government spends goes on this. We are a nation hooked on welfare. Our spending on social security has doubled since the end of WWII. This takes us nicely into another of those Big Political Questions: 'How on earth are we going to stop spending £130 billion a year on social security?' One to put to the door-to-door canvassers at election time, perhaps. Slashing people's dole money, or pensions, or cancelling benefits, would of course be unthinkable. But then again, when Tony Blair was trying to work out how to save money, he told an expert – Labour MP Frank Field – to do just that. 'Think the unthinkable,' he said. So Frank Field did. He came up with various ways of cutting zillions of pounds from our social-security budget. He was fired.

The next biggest money pit is the NHS. In 2003, spending on health amounted to £1,100 for every person in this country. You could be fit as a fiddle, but you individually – just you – still spend around a grand a year on the National Health Service. You also spend £900 a year on education. And £400 each on defence and law and order.

The poor relation in all this, you may not be surprised to learn, is transport. Over the years, it's fallen steadily to the bottom of the government's shopping list. In 1993 they bunged just 2 per cent of the national kitty on it. By the end of the 1990s they'd slashed even that by half. Politicians on both sides had stopped seeing it as a priority, obviously. (And realised there were no votes in it.)

The person to blame – or praise, depending on your point of view – for the amount of money we spend on things like benefits and the NHS is William Henry Beveridge. He pretty much invented the modern welfare state when, in 1942, he came up with the Beveridge Report. No, not the name of an investigative TV show, but something that led to the formation of the NHS in 1948. It was Beveridge who first had the idea that the welfare state should always be there for us, from the cradle to the grave. And we've been shelling out more and more on it ever since. The figures are staggering, and excellent for causing arguments. Soon we will, proportionately, be spending *ten times* more on health than we were in 1950.

More Big Political Questions: 'Is all this money being spent efficiently, or are we just pouring billions and billions of pounds into a big black hole?' 'Should we be encouraging more people to pay for their own health care?' 'Why should fit, healthy non-smokers have money taken off them, to pay for medical treatment for smokers?' 'Should there be free NHS care only for those who *really* need it?'

Mind you, it could be worse. We could be Scandinavian. Overall, the Swedes pay roughly 40 per cent more in tax than us. And the Danes, Finns and Norwegians aren't far behind. In fact, we are classed, believe it or not, as being a relatively low tax country, compared to the rest of Europe.

In the year 2000, out of the 30 largest industrial nations in the world, we came 18th in terms of rates of tax. The 12 countries who paid less tax than us included Australia, America and, right at the bottom – paying less than half what we do (don't ask me why) – Mexico.

The trick for any government, clearly, is to get the balance right. We are back in the realms of plucking goose feathers without too much hissing here. Obviously, we are always going to have to pay something. As economists say, tax is the instrument that helps a society achieve its goals. (Sounds good, doesn't it? I nicked it off the net.) But if you charge too much, it will be counterproductive. You will penalise the very people you should be trying to reward, such as risk takers, entrepreneurs and innovators. Think about it. If a country charges 98 per cent income tax, no one will want to pay. They'll emigrate, or start stuffing wads of cash under the floorboards. But make it 35 per cent, say, and pretty much everyone will cough up.

But what can you do if you think the government has got the balance wrong? Well, you could take inspiration from the French, and get awkeard. An anti-tax group over there reckoned taxes were too high and that the French government wasn't spending the revenue sensibly. So they took out newspaper adverts to celebrate Tax Liberation Day. The date was 16 July – because they'd worked out that French people have to work from the start of the year until that date before their

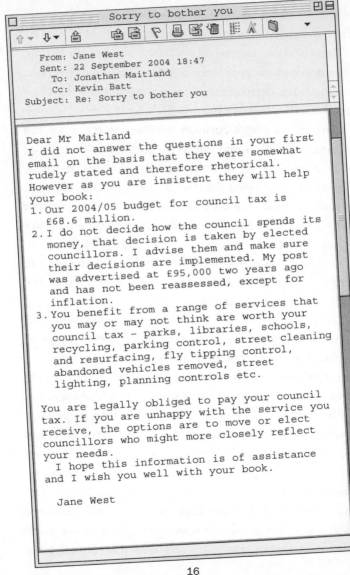

Sorry to bother you

From: Jane West
Sent: 22 September 2004 18:47
To: Jonathan Maitland
Cc: Kevin Batt
Subject: Re: Sorry to bother you

Dear Mr Maitland
I did not answer the questions in your first
email on the basis that they were somewhat
rudely stated and therefore rhetorical.
However as you are insistent they will help
your book:
1. Our 2004/05 budget for council tax is
   £68.6 million.
2. I do not decide how the council spends its
   money, that decision is taken by elected
   councillors. I advise them and make sure
   their decisions are implemented. My post
   was advertised at £95,000 two years ago
   and has not been reassessed, except for
   inflation.
3. You benefit from a range of services that
   you may or may not think are worth your
   council tax – parks, libraries, schools,
   recycling, parking control, street cleaning
   and resurfacing, fly tipping control,
   abandoned vehicles removed, street
   lighting, planning controls etc.

You are legally obliged to pay your council
tax. If you are unhappy with the service you
receive, the options are to move or elect
councillors who might more closely reflect
your needs.
   I hope this information is of assistance
and I wish you well with your book.

   Jane West

wages actually go into their own pockets, as opposed to the government's.

There are also dozens of small taxpayer groups all over France, getting stroppy and saying, 'Oi, that's our money you're spending.' (In French.) One campaign is led by a retired IBM worker called Michel Vergnaud. He only got into it, he said, out of curiosity. But he quickly found that local taxes in his home city of Lyons had been rising at three times the rate of inflation. 'They are not spending out of need,' fumed Monsieur Vergnaud, 'but simply because they have the tax revenue.' So he took the city, and Rhone regional authorities, to court. He won. Officials in both bureaucracies now have to work longer hours.

Hmm. This rings a bell. In Britain, central government administration costs have risen by 40 per cent in five years. That's also three times the rate of inflation. How can this have happened? Try asking the Scots. Their new Parliament building in Edinburgh cost £400 million at the last count. But the original estimate was – get this – just £50 million. That means that £350 million worth of tax payers' money has been squandered. Unbelievable!

The trouble is – and this won't come as a huge surprise to you – some of those who govern us just aren't up to the job. This is especially true of local councils. My mate, who has worked for a London council for 18 years, told me what goes on in his: 'The councillors spend hours haggling over a five hundred quid overspend on the bins but then they go and wave a three million pound development through, on the

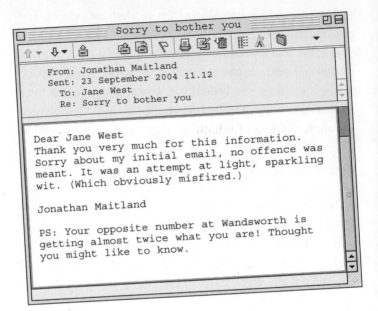

Sorry to bother you

From: Jonathan Maitland
Sent: 23 September 2004 11.12
To: Jane West
Re: Sorry to bother you

Dear Jane West
Thank you very much for this information.
Sorry about my initial email, no offence was
meant. It was an attempt at light, sparkling
wit. (Which obviously misfired.)

Jonathan Maitland

PS: Your opposite number at Wandsworth is
getting almost twice what you are! Thought
you might like to know.

nod, just like that … it's scary. You've got to ask
yourself how many mistakes they make. If a big
company doing work for them bunged fifty grand
extra on the bill, just for the sake of it, would they
ever notice?'

Donald J. Johnston of the Organisation for Economic
Cooperation and Development (OECD) is a very big
cheese in the economic world. He has talked a lot about
this very point – ie how our money gets spent. He says
that our society can be made better and closer, through
what he terms 'transparent and well-designed taxation'.

Hello. 'Transparent taxation'. In other words, we

have a choice. We can say: 'Here's the cheque. Now go and spend it.' Or, we can complain more. I know which option I prefer.

I think I have reached a conclusion. Paying tax is the penalty – or if you prefer, the privilege – that comes with living in a civilised, caring 'n' sharing democracy like ours. Talking of which...

CHAPTER TWO

How it all Started

Democracy started in Shepherd's Bush on Tuesday, 13 July 2004, at 8.46am – for me, at any rate. That's when I got on a 94 bus to the Houses of Parliament to see a bloke called Philip Norton, who probably knows more about that particular subject than anyone else in the world. Text books, however, put the start of democracy at some 2,500 years earlier.

Like most people, if invited to talk for one minute without hesitation, deviation or repetition on the origins of British democracy I would feel a sudden urge to rearrange my sock drawer or, if feeling brave, would offer: 'Er... Magna Carta? The Greeks? Oliver Cromwell?' before admitting defeat. That has to change. But don't worry, this is no constitutional snoozefest of a chapter. You'll be through it in less than 20 minutes. Which is how long it took me to get to Westminster, the Houses of Parliament and Philip Norton.

One small obstacle stood in my way: I didn't know what he looked like. James, who makes political TV programmes, has impeccable contacts and is helping me research this book, told me to look out for a balding, middle-aged man with glasses. But doing that at the House of Commons is like trying to find someone in a red scarf at a Manchester United game.

Phillip – his official title is actually Lord Norton of Louth – told me in an email to meet him outside the Wilson Room. Once there, I saw someone who looked like he might be Lord Phil talking to a man who looked suspiciously like a very old Geoffrey Howe, the former

Foreign Secretary. I didn't want to interrupt them, so I asked the uniformed policeman guarding the door to the Wilson Room if that was Lord Norton of Louth over there, and was that really Geoffrey Howe he was with, or a lookalike?

It was indeed the Phil 'n' Geoff show.

I asked the policeman what they were here for.

'It's an inquiry. Into inquiries.'

No hint of a smile. He was either great at deadpanning or he had no sense of humour.

'What? This is an inquiry into inquiries?'

'Yes sir.'

'Right. Thanks.'

Welcome to British democracy!

Geoffrey Howe is the man whose speaking style was once famously compared to a dead sheep. The next 90 minutes made me realise why: hard as I tried, I managed to hear only 40 per cent of what he was saying. It was like listening to a generator. Three MPs took it in turns to quiz Geoffrey and Lord Phil about inquiries – when they should be called, who should sit on them, etc. If British democracy is a 900-year-old oak tree, then this meeting was the tip of a leaf on the end of one of the tree's thousand branches. Hence my first question to Lord Phil, as he poured tea out of the House of Commons embossed pot in one of Westminster's many tea rooms:

'Who planted the acorn?'

Lord Phil tensed and flexed a bit, like an athlete limbering up for a big race.

'Aha. You want a free lesson. Right. Well, it was the Greeks. Yes, the Greeks.'

We were off. According to Lord Phil, in about the fifth century BC something happened which, in the words of political boffin Professor Robert Dahl, was 'As important as the invention of the wheel or the discovery of the New World.'

About a century later, the Greek philosopher Aristotle wrote a book about what had gone on, called *Politics*. It's thanks to him – the world's first ever political journalist – that we have a reasonable idea of how democracy was born. Athens, Aristotle tells us, was the blueprint. Around four times a month, the people would meet on the slopes of a small hill close to the Acropolis to discuss the issues of the day. This gathering was known as the Assembly. Normally around seven thousand of them got together. It was a very pure form of democracy: everything was done in the open and everyone could see what everyone else was doing. And everyone played an active part.

At this time, said Aristotle, Greece wasn't a country, but an area containing a number of independent cities, or *polis* – the origin of the word 'politics'. Each city, or *polis*, had to devise a system of getting things done, and so they copied Athens. The Assemblies weren't exactly representative, though: no women, slaves, peasants, children or foreigners. It was men only. But then they could hardly be politically correct – they'd only just invented politics.

All of a sudden, you had the ancient Greek equivalent of lots of local parliaments. Very big local parliaments. Curiously, Plato, who was around at the same time as Aristotle, decided that the ideal number of people for a *polis* was 5,040 men. (Don't ask me why.) Both Aristotle and Plato agreed that for these mini democracies to work well, everyone had to know each other. There was no distinction, back then, between private and public life: both were one and the same. The public world was joined with the private world.

Often, the (exclusively male) citizens didn't use voting as a way of deciding things. After much discussion, a general agreement, or consensus, would be reached. Voting was only a last resort. After a while, though, for obvious reasons, it was clear there were some things this group of a few thousand citizens couldn't do together. Such as draw up an agenda, organise meetings and announce decisions. So they elected officials to do that for them. There were usually around five hundred of these and they were known as the Council. And so democracy was born.

The British, however, didn't catch a whiff of this for around 1,600 years. We felt our first democratic throbbings, Lord Phil told me, at around the time of King John. Back in the early 1200s, the king realised he couldn't do it all by himself. So he decided to consult a few other people – ie big cheeses in the Church and landowners – about things such as laws, wars and taxes. Somebody then decided that this arrangement was going well, and that they had better write it down before the king changed his mind – so they did, in 1215, in a document called Magna Carta. For historical purposes, democracy in Britain had to start somewhere, so it started there.

What happened in 1215 was momentous. Back then, before he signed Magna Carta, King John was a bit like Alex Ferguson. He alone had total control over all the important stuff: team selection, tactics, training methods, the lot. The Manchester United supporters – ie ordinary people – didn't get a look-in. But when King John put his name to Magna Carta, it was like Fergie formally agreeing, in writing, to consult senior members of the team at all times and on all occasions. From that day on, the power started to slip away from the top very slowly indeed, over a very long period of time, until we got to where we are today. Now, ultimate power belongs, in theory at least, to those at the bottom – ie the people. But that process took more than seven hundred years, and there were some monumental power struggles on the way.

A democracy is a system of government in which all the adults in a society, with few exceptions, are allowed a free and fair vote. In Britain, that didn't happen until the 20th century. But voting of a highly disorganised and usually corrupt kind has actually been taking place in Britain since the 13th century. Mind you, ballot papers, electoral rolls and percentage swings played little part in these early, cack-handed attempts at democracy. But there were elements, at least, of 'popular' and 'voting' about what was going on.

27

It worked like this: once word got to Chichester, say, that the king wanted a couple of local bigwigs to help him out, all the local landowners (perhaps fifty of them, perhaps five hundred) would get together in the town square and decide who should be nominated. After much discussion, ale-glugging and chicken leg-scoffing, a winner of sorts would emerge. The medieval Member of Parlement (as it was known then) had duly been elected.

'It was more of a selection than an election,' said Lord Phil, pouring more tea. 'People didn't particularly want to be voted up to Parliament, like they do today; there was a bit of the short straw about it.' But over the next 300 years, as the various kings (and Queen Elizabeth I) found themselves becoming more and more dependent on the support of Parliament, these medieval MPs started to quite fancy the trip to London.

The trouble is, there were no hard-and-fast rules about whether it was the monarch or Parliament that had ultimate control. If the king wanted to raise a million pounds in tax from the people, and Parliament thought that was too much, whose will would prevail? No one had written down the rules for what had become a game of very high stakes; there was bound to be trouble.

And there was, in the form of the great Civil War of 1642–9. Everyone knows you should never lose your head in an argument, but that is exactly what happened to King Charles I, courtesy of Oliver Cromwell. This plunged Britain into a strange democratic no-man's-land for 11 years. It wasn't a democracy; it wasn't a monarchy;

it was a military dictatorship. And it didn't work. Soon there was a king back on the throne (Charles II) and we were back to the old routine: one almighty wrestling match between the monarchy and Parliament. It was a contest only one side could win. This was because: a) it was very uneven – ie one man (plus a bunch of cronies) against the rest; and b) the king was, more often than not, thick. James I for instance was a stupid, crotch-scratching egomaniac with a tongue so big it hung out of his mouth. (Not unlike a Premiership footballer.)

This kingly stupidity and lack of judgement reached a critical point in 1688 – another date for your diaries. Politically, this was A Big Year, the year that Parliament wrestled the monarchy to the floor, got it in a headlock and the fight was finally called off for good. For it was in 1688 that James II painted himself, and the monarchy, into a corner. He had been going around telling everyone who would listen that he was put on the throne by God – a concept known as 'ruling by divine right' – and therefore everyone had to obey him. Not surprisingly, Parliament told James that he was bonkers and ordered him to get out of the country. In a rare moment of good judgement James realised they were serious and did just that. Parliament then invited William and Mary of Orange over from the Netherlands to rule in James' place. In that moment, things changed for ever. The new rulers now owed their position to Parliament, not the other way round, and the question of who was truly in charge would never arise again.

But it wasn't as if Britain suddenly became a model democracy overnight. It practised a crooked and hideously unrepresentative system: in the 18th and early 19th centuries, only 2 per cent of the country could vote. That resulted in some ludicrously unfair situations, especially when big cities such as Manchester and Birmingham began to spring up during the Industrial Revolution. It wasn't unusual for small, corrupt places with just ten people in them – so-called 'rotten boroughs' – to send not one, but two representatives up to Parliament. The huge new centres of population on the other hand, had no votes, and no MPs. Politically, they didn't exist.

All this inspired the Reform Act of 1832, which shone the bright, burning torch of electoral choice where once there had been democratic darkness (sorry about that). This Act marked the moment that British democracy truly started to blossom. It was the first proper attempt to sort out an organised system of voting, and it led to our first ever general election, which took place later that year. The torch didn't shine everywhere, though: the Act gave only 7 per cent of the nation the vote. The next Reform Act, passed 35 years later, carried on where the first one had left off and more than doubled the electoral roll. But even then, four-fifths of the population still couldn't join the party, let alone vote for one.

Even so, millions had caught a glimpse of the light, and wanted it to shine on them; the democratic genie was out of the bottle. Over the next few decades, more and more people became enfranchised. Finally, in 1928, British democracy became the glorious oak tree it is today, when women were given the same voting rights as men. From that day on, anyone over 21 could do it. Hallelujah.

It was time to go. I thanked Lord Phil for giving me a history of the democratic world in three and a half cups, and headed for Westminster tube station – which, helpfully, is directly connected to the Houses of Parliament by an underground walkway. Not many people know that. It had indeed been a day of discovery. On the way home, a thought struck me. Millions of British people have given their lives for democracy. They died so that we could vote. So how come millions of us *aren't*? I'm glad I asked me that...

CHAPTER THREE

Why Aren't we Voting and Does it Matter Anyway?

I can see a pattern forming. Three weeks into the writing of this book, and I am with yet another bald, middle-aged man with glasses. This one is sitting in an office in Elephant and Castle, one of the grimmest parts of London, and has the added bonus of an American accent. His name is Bob Worcester.

Everything about Bob says 'favourite uncle'. His manner, his smile and his slow, kindly 'Let me explain this to you, sonny' tone of voice. If Bob had a white beard, a baggy red suit and a sack on his back, he'd make a great Father Christmas.

You probably won't have heard of Bob Worcester, but you might know the company he started. MORI (Market and Opinion Research Institute) carries out opinion polls and has done very well indeed out of them, thank you very much. In fact, if Uncle Bob wanted to, he could play Father Christmas to the whole of Elephant and Castle, as the company he founded is now worth more than £50 million. No wonder he looks happy.

Worcester makes, if you'll excuse the pun, a great source when it comes to voting. He wrote the book. Literally. The jauntily titled *The History and Methodology of Political Opinion Polling*. He is the perfect person to put the question at the top of this page. So I do just that. But first, we need to establish if low voter turnout really is the biggest threat to British democracy since Hitler put his jackboots on. So we do what Uncle Bob does best: talk percentages.

A lot of people in this country aren't voting, Uncle Bob tells me. When he started in this game, more than eight out of ten of us voted. At the last election less than six out of ten did. That's a drop of a quarter. It means that, overall, 18 million people didn't vote. Eighteen million people.

Young people, those under 24, were the worst offenders, if that's the right word. Less than 40 per cent of them voted in 2001. Forgive me for stating the obvious, but that means more than 60 per cent of young people didn't vote last time around. That's pretty startling. Why didn't they? Was it because they couldn't be arsed and were too busy binge drinking, wearing hoods and downloading music on to iPods?

Apparently not. Uncle Bob says it wasn't apathy, but alienation. An awful lot of young people these days just don't like politics or politicians. They're too boring, too remote: they're not relevant. Politics isn't very exciting any more. I know that's a strange thing to say: it implies that politics *was* exciting, once upon a time. That might be a difficult concept to grasp. But exciting it was.

Take the election of 1974, and what led up to it. I was fat, 12 years old and at an all-boys prep school. It was in the middle of nowhere. But I still remember the atmosphere generated by the almighty political battle of the time, despite being far more interested in the school tuck shop than politics. Depending on your point of view, it was a good-versus-evil-type thing. In the red corner were the working class, striking miners and the

Labour Party. In the blue corner were the Tory government, the middle classes and posh people. It was a fight to the death. Because of the miners' strike, the government had put everyone on a three-day week to save energy. There were power cuts of up to nine hours a day. And voters took to the polling booths, big time. Because they felt compelled to. Because it felt like it really mattered.

As a result, eight out of ten people voted. That's a *third* more than in 2001. But then again, they had more reasons to vote: there was more at stake. Nowadays, it's different. For a start, it's hard to tell the teams apart. Both parties want pretty much the same things – good schools, better hospitals and less crime. And they'd both charge us roughly the same rates of tax for them. In other words, whoever you vote for, you'll end up with the same thing. So why bother?

These days however, if you're young, into politics and want excitement, the last thing on your mind is voting. You want to get involved. And that means joining a pressure group or a single-issue party. If you don't believe me, look at the numbers. The Royal Society for the Protection of Birds now has more than a million fully paid-up, committed members. That's more than all the political parties in Britain put together. Of that million, more than 150,000 are young people. Other pressure groups, such as the World Wildlife Fund and Friends of the Earth, are seeing the same thing.

You don't have to be Sherlock Holmes to work out why

your average twentysomething would rather join a pressure group, or go on a demo, than vote. After all, direct action is a lot more – er – direct. And fun. Invading the floor of the House of Commons, or climbing a tree and refusing to come down, is a lot more exciting, relevant and connected than voting for someone you haven't even met.

In other words, a lot of young people *are* interested in politics, massively – they're just not interested in voting. Take Isaac Ferry, teenage son of Bryan, the crooning lounge lizard who used to front Roxy Music. Isaac, who's keen on hunting, got suspended from the poshest public school in the land, Eton, in 2002. He'd allegedly sent an abusive email to a well-known badger lover and environmentalist, which ran thus:

You are a fucking looser. Why don't you stop waisting your time and get a proper job/hobby, you cunt?

What's interesting here is: a) it must have made his dad wonder whether Eton's £16,488-a-year school fees included the cost of spelling lessons; and b) it suggests that Isaac and many thousands like him do indeed have political priorities, but voting isn't high among them. They're far more committed to whatever cause it is they are committed to. How's voting going to help them achieve their aims, when they can use more direct methods?

The Ferry family are godsends when it comes to backing up this argument, because it was Isaac's brother, Otis, who managed the spectacular coup of storming the floor of the House of Commons in 2004. Again, they were protesting about a ban on hunting. Interestingly, the grandfather of Isaac and Otis was a coal miner. I think that's significant (but I'm not sure why).

This isn't some airy-fairy theory dreamed up in my garden shed: advertisers have also sussed that kids are well into politics with a small 'p'. Polo Ralph Lauren, one of the biggest fashion brands around, have launched GIVE jeans – a cut of the revenue goes to politically aware charities. Cynical maybe, but revealing. Well-hip fashion brands Phat Farm and Drunknmunky (I'm a British Home Stores man myself) are doing the same. The former campaigns for economic justice for black people, the latter against mass manufacturing.

There are other reasons why we're not voting. I like the one that says we're simply too intelligent and sophisticated. (It makes sense, don't worry.) The argument, which political boffins call the 'theory of rationality', goes like this. We don't like wasting our time these days. We're also better informed, so we know what's going on. We look at the polls, and see that our preferred party is bound to win the election. We realise we don't actually *need* to vote, so we don't. We let others do it for us. Likewise if our preferred party looks like losing: we know our vote won't change anything, so we stay at home.

Here's another reason why we don't vote. It can be summed up in one date: 1990. The year when loads of Britons hit the streets, and quite a few policemen, during riots over the Conservative Party's hated poll tax. Curiously, the effect of all that seething discontent was not, as you might imagine, to turn people off the Tories, whose policy it was. Instead, it made a whole generation of people pissed off with politics, and politicians, in general. Research shows that people took it out on the system: they became too disillusioned to vote. Exactly why this happened – why they blamed politics generally, rather than the Tories in particular – is beyond me and apparently it's all to do with the unique character of the British people.

But the best reason why lots of us don't vote, I reckon, is the practical one. Put simply, voting is bloody inconvenient. I have dug out some figures that make very interesting reading. Half of those who didn't vote last time said it was simply because they couldn't make it to the polling booth on that particular day. Or they were away. Or they hadn't received their polling card. The figures show that around 10 million people wanted to vote, but for various workaday reasons, they didn't.

Once you factor that in, the whole picture looks very different. Basically, if it hadn't been for our useless voting system, the turnout at the last election might have been higher than at any time in the last hundred years. It could have been more than 80 per cent.

The problem is simple. Our voting system hasn't changed in more than 170 years. It has failed dismally to keep up with the times. When they held the first ever General Election in 1832, it was based on paper and ink. Now, in the era of the internet and mobiles, it still is. We may be in the 21st century but our voting system belongs to the 19th.

If we'd been able to use phones at the last election it would have made a massive difference. Amazingly, two-thirds of those who didn't vote in 2001 say that if they'd been allowed to do it by phone, they would have. That means as many as 12 million additional votes could have been cast. Which means we could have had a completely different result. Maybe that's why those in power haven't updated the system: they're scared of what the changes might bring.

Yes, there is an issue of security: if we all voted by mobile phone there might be fraud. But that's not a good reason for not looking into this option. It could also make a big difference if voting didn't take place on a busy weekday. Elections happen on a Thursday. Why not hold them over a three- or four-day period? Or on a Sunday?

Our system of registering people to vote is also a bit rubbish. You can't vote unless you're registered. And you have to re-register every year. But the figures show that many people don't know that. Even the ones that do, think you can only re-register at a certain time, which is wrong: you can do it whenever you like.

So hold the front page. The experts and the media have got it wrong. When Peter Hain, a Labour government bigwig, recently put the shockingly low turnout of 2001 down to alienation and apathy among voters, he should have blamed the lack of a 'vote now' button on their Nokia 5210s.

That's why it's so misleading to go around quoting the statistic that more young people voted in *Big Brother* than they did in the last General Election. That's only half the story. Lots of young people voted in *Big Brother* because it was quick, convenient and they didn't have to leave their couches. Given the opportunity they would do the same at a general election.

Take my wife. It's lazy, I know, quoting so close to home, but she's a corking example of everything I've just been saying. She didn't vote in 2001, even though she wanted to. But by the time she'd made breakfast for the kids, taken them to school, cleaned the house, done the shopping, paid the bills, returned the library books, been for a swim, met her mate Julia for coffee in Ravenscourt Park, read *The Times*, marked her students' mock exam papers, sorted out the kids' sock drawer, picked the kids up from school, made them tea, watched a bit of TV and cooked dinner, she realised it was too late. The location of the polling booths was also a problem. Too far to walk, too short to drive, too difficult to park. And she cares about politics: she went on the Stop The War march in 2003, likes foreign affairs and reads a big newspaper.

But if she'd been able to use her mobile, she'd have voted. Then again, she didn't feel compelled to because she knew there could only be two outcomes, neither of which would change her life. Whoever got in, things would carry on more or less the same.

When my wife's parents were her age, though, they never missed a chance to vote. Because it really mattered. My wife's mum used to say she'd gladly walk two miles in her bare feet to find a can of beans that was 2p cheaper. In 1974, Labour Chancellor Denis Healey was proposing a top rate of tax of 98p in the pound. The Tories wanted it to be 40p. The difference between the two parties represented an awful lot of a) baked beans and b) reasons to vote.

There are other reasons why quite a few British people don't vote, of course: because they're not allowed to. Nutters, for example, aren't eligible. The following also have no voting rights: peers and peeresses in the House of Lords, foreign nationals, the criminally insane, people in prison and under-18s. So if your name is Lord Boris Bereznikov and you are reading this in the under-18s wing for the completely bonkers at Wormwood Scrubs, don't go near a polling booth.

The trouble is, no one's taken the time to explain all this to politicians, which is why many of them think it's a scandal that not enough of us are voting. One or two even reckon it should be made compulsory. In fact, in some countries it is.

43

Pub quiz anoraks take note: there are 33 countries with mandatory voting laws, including Belgium, Australia, Fiji, Luxembourg and Cyprus. You don't get bunged in jail in these places if you don't vote, though. In Australia, for example, they write you a letter asking why you didn't show. If you come up with a good reason, they let you off. If you don't have one, and you're unlucky, you might get a $50 fine. In Italy, they have a law – rarely used now – whereby non-voters get their names plastered all over public notice boards, with DID NOT VOTE stamped next to it. Named and shamed!

However, those sorts of penalties aren't going to happen here. Compulsory voting isn't really a runner. And here's why:

1. No one important wants it.
2. Forcing people to vote just isn't very British, you know.
3. Our right *not* to vote is every bit as valuable as our right to vote. Not voting can be just as big a political statement as voting.
4. Enforcement problems. What are you going to do if a million people don't vote – bung them in jail?
5. It's not our fault we're not voting, it's the politicians'. Forcing us to vote isn't very healthy for democracy and doesn't address the real problem.

There's quite an attractive halfway house, though, which you might like the sound of. They could bribe us. The authorities did this in ancient Greece. In 392BC they paid people three obols to vote – the equivalent of a quarter of a day's pay. It's even been suggested that people should be given a free lottery ticket in return for voting. Or that they should get a reduction in their council tax of between £5 and £20. It would work for me.

* * * * *

Right, we've got that out of the way. On to the next question. Does it *matter*, these days, if fewer of us vote? Uncle Bob, still smiling benignly across the table from me, reckons it does. If the turnout fell to 50 per cent – and the way things are going, he says, it easily could – it would matter hugely. If voting falls to that level, he claims, there might be a hung parliament, ie Labour and the Tories would be roughly neck and neck. Because of the way our voting system works – more of which later – minority parties would hold the balance of power. Eek! In Uncle Bob's opinion that means nasty parties like the British National Party (BNP) would be able to hold everyone to ransom. A vicious git could become PM and all ethnic minorities would be deported.

Not so fast, Uncle Bob. The BNP would have to get around 25,000 votes in one constituency to get just one seat in Parliament. And that's just the one seat. Out of a current total of 659. I know there are a lot of stupid, thick racists around, but there aren't that many in one place at one time, unless you happen to be at a football match in Spain, of course.

The BNP have occasionally managed to leave the odd toe print, I know. In the 2002 local elections in Burnley they got a few hundred votes and three seats on the council. But it wasn't as big a deal as the media made out. They didn't get any real power in Burnley – ie enough to make policy or influence events – they merely got a platform to air their views. Which isn't a bad thing, arguably, as once BNP types are out in the open, everyone gets to see how ludicrous they are. And anyway, the BNP only managed to win those seats because the voting system for local elections favours minority parties; that's not the case at general elections.

So the answer to the big question is: no. It doesn't really matter if we don't vote. If turnouts keep falling, democracy won't suddenly die and Adolf Hitler won't take over. The British just aren't like that. And in the unlikely event that a gang of weirdoes/extremists/genocidal maniacs did suddenly loom on the horizon, we'd all be down the voting booths in a flash anyway.

It is time for me to say goodbye to Uncle Bob. He has researchers to brief, percentages to sling, books to write. As a leaving present he gives me a copy of one. It's called *We British*. Leafing through it on the tube on the way home, another post-interview thought occurs to me. Maybe the real reason why politicians want us to vote more is this: they simply can't bear the fact that more and more of us are ignoring them.

And anyway, there's a bright side to all this: 25 million of us, at the last count, *do* vote. The question is...

CHAPTER FOUR

Why do we Vote the Way we do?

There's a long and a short answer to that. The short one first: for an awful lot of people – the most influential, key voters in Britain, in fact – it's all down to just two things. How our leaders look, and what they're like on TV. Many consequences flow from that. One is that a balding ginger gnome like Robin Cook has as much chance of being Prime Minister as a one-legged man has of winning an arse-kicking contest. Harsh, but true. Even Mr Cook himself admitted this, when the leadership of the Labour Party came up for grabs. 'Why don't you go for it?' colleagues urged him. 'Because I'm too much of a dog on TV,' was, in effect, his reply.

Now for the slightly longer answer. There are other reasons why we vote the way we do, apart from TV. One important factor is our parents, especially our fathers. Two researchers called David Butler and Donald Stokes discovered this, through a series of studies into voting habits, in 1969. If our dad voted Tory, then there's a good chance we will, too. Of course, not everyone votes Tory simply because their parents did: it's a lot more complex than that. But if you made up a list of the deciding factors, parental voting habits – surprisingly – would be at the top.

There are other prevailing winds when it comes to the great weather vane of voting. One is class. The working classes – or at least those that still exist – are much more likely to vote Labour. The other is housing: people who bought their council homes courtesy of Mrs Thatcher are still much more likely to vote Tory.

But what's crucial here are the numbers involved. For

the reasons I've just given, 80 per cent of us are completely fixed in our voting habits. In other words, 80 per cent of us will vote the same way next time, as we did last time. Even if our preferred party proposes to make eating cheese a criminal offence, we will continue to support them.

But that, my dear Watson, leaves 20 per cent of voters who are undecided. In real numbers, that's a million people. These – roll on the drums, please – are the 'floating voters'. 'Promiscuous voters' might be more accurate, though, as these people can't decide who to get into bed with next. For our purposes, they are The Voters Who Are So Crucial You Wouldn't Believe It. That's because these million people hold the political future of this country in their hands. If most of them vote Tory at the next election, the Tories will win, massively. If most vote Labour, then Labour will walk it, big time. It's a quirk of our electoral system. These million people – less than 2 per cent of the population of the entire country – have, between them, the power to deliver a massive 180-seat majority for either of the main parties.

Clearly, then, these million people are absolutely crucial. And the parties know it. Because my mate Uncle Bob, no less, told them. He told John Smith, the late Labour leader, before the General Election in 1992. The moment Uncle Bob explained about the Voters Who Are So Crucial You Wouldn't Believe It, he says, he saw the light bulb go on over Smith's head. 'Only a million?' said the politician. 'Hell! We can bribe them!'

'The trouble was,' says Uncle Bob, 'he couldn't find them – he didn't know who they were, or where.'

Uncle Bob and his chums have managed to find out one very important thing about The Voters Who Are So Crucial You Wouldn't Believe It, though. Most of them – 60 per cent, in fact, which is more than enough to swing an election decisively – vote on the basis of one thing: a politician's image. You thought elections were decided on health, education and transport? Yes, up to a point. But there are more decisive issues, I'm afraid. For health, education and transport, read hair, elocution and teeth.

That means the next election, and the one after that, will be decided by people like Marion McGowan, a gentle lady in her 60s, from Evesham. When you ask Marion why she votes a certain way, she says: 'Do you know, there's just… something about him.'

Aha. That all-important 'something'. But what is it, exactly? After all, if you could define it and bottle it, you'd have the keys to the kingdom, the secret of never-ending political success. But you can't. That something – the X-factor, the thing that makes a leader want you to vote for him or her – is impossible to describe accurately. At the moment, says Marion, there's no one who's really got it. And according to her, there is someone who definitely hasn't: 'That Tony Blair. Goodness, he makes me cringe. All that idiot grinning, with the jeans and the coffee mug. We don't want to see our prime minister like that, we want him in a suit and tie.' Clearly, there are a lot of people who disagree with Marion: for them, the jeans, the idiot grinning and the coffee mug are a plus, not a minus. But what she says is helpful, because although you can't really define what that something *is*, you can say what it *isn't*.

And one thing it definitely isn't − prospective prime ministers please take note − is a tendency to try and score political points at every opportunity. MORI's Uncle Bob regularly puts a load of The Voters Who Are So Crucial You Wouldn't Believe It into a room and shows them tapes of various politicians in action in the House of Commons. Last time out the tapes featured Tony Blair and Michael Howard. Blair scored well; Howard didn't. The Voters Who Are So Crucial reckoned Howard was too combative. He looked like he was arguing the toss about everything just for the sake of it. As a result, The Voters Who Are So Crucial were less likely to vote for him. Blair on the other hand, rose above the fray. Politicians trying to achieve that all-important statesmanlike quality, take note.

You might not be able to define that certain 'something', then, but that hasn't stopped countless politicians trying to acquire it. It's difficult, of course: you can't force people to like you or respect you. It's not a science, it's an inexact art − all down to whims, instincts and gut reactions. But as I said, that hasn't put politicians off. Ambitious ones know that possibly the most effective way to improve their image, and get a head start in the Marion McGowan 'There's something about him' stakes, is to speak well.

Interestingly, even the grimmest, dullest, public speaker

(come in Geoffrey Howe) can become a bit of a star if they follow a few basic rules. This was proved, rather entertainingly, when Ann Brennan, a complete unknown, spoke at the SDP conference in 1984. (The SDP later merged with the Liberal Party to form the Liberal Democrats.) In a unique experiment, Ann was given a checklist of things to do by a bloke called Max Atkinson. He'd spent years working out what made a good speaker, and had written a book on it. She followed every bit of his advice, to the letter. It worked a treat. She ended up getting so much applause from the audience that she ran out of time. In fact, she was the only rank-and-file party member who got a standing ovation that year.

Some of the things Max Atkinson tells politicians to do may be a bit obvious, but they're worth listing, so here goes:

1. DO SINCERITY WELL

If you can fake this, you're halfway there. So bin your script if possible. Learn it if you can, or use a giant transparent autocue – a so-called 'sincerity board' that has your words on it. You will be able to see the words, but the audience won't. Trouble is, some people are getting wise to this trick. So, if you're canny, you'll stroll around the stage during your speech to make it look like you don't have autocue. You fox!

2. LOOK THEM IN THE EYE

Always keep eye contact with your audience. This means not wearing glasses. That's why Adolf Hitler never went to Specsavers: he made sure he was never seen, or photographed in public, wearing spectacles.

3. MAKE GESTURES

Use your arms, hands and fingers to make a point. This is important for conveying passion. But don't over-egg it or you'll end up doing a bad windmill impersonation.

4. USE LISTS OF THREE

Abraham Lincoln cottoned on to this more than 140 years ago, in the line: 'Government of the people, by the people, for the people.' This technique is termed a 'clap trap' – ie a trick deliberately used to attract applause. If you get the timing right, and use a rising inflection at the end of your list, you will be guaranteed a round of applause lasting from seven to nine seconds. Apparently.

5. USE 'INNER CONTRASTS'

Ideally, these should be contained in neat, short sentences. For example: 'Ask not what your country can do for you. Ask what you can do for your country.' The President of the USA, John F. Kennedy, said this in 1961. It is another example of a 'clap trap'.

6. BLOW YOUR OWN TRUMPET AND SLAG THE OTHERS OFF

... preferably at the same time – eg 'We are the party of youth, vigour and new ideas. They are fat, complacent has-beens.' Believe me, it works. When Max Atkinson

55

analysed 100 bursts of applause at party conferences he found that nearly 90 per cent of them followed what he called 'positive evaluations of "us" or negative evaluations of "them".'

7. LOWER THE TONE

I don't mean swear a lot, I mean go down a few octaves. Especially if you're female. Mrs Thatcher took lessons from a voice tutor at the National Theatre, which included special humming exercises. She managed to drop her pitch by 46 Hz, almost half the difference in pitch between male and female voices. She also slowed down her delivery. It worked. She went from a shrill semi-shriek to sounding prime ministerial and in control.

8. TALK OVER THE APPLAUSE

Once the audience begins to clap, don't wait for the applause to die down. Start talking over the top of it, after about three or four seconds. This makes it look as if you are not expecting the applause, and that what you have to say is more important than mere clapping.

As I say, some of these are a bit obvious. But it doesn't do any harm to know when we're having out buttons pushed.

Admittedly, it's not the hardest thing in the world to get a round of applause at party conferences. You could read from the phone book and get an ovation, provided you got the timing and inflections right:

'AAA Emergency Plumbers.' (Pause.)

'*They* rip you off.' (Pause. Go up a tone. Point to yourself using both forefingers.)

'*We* won't.' (Applause comes. Wait for three seconds. Then talk over it.)

'Ring 0870 909090 now!' (Audience goes bonkers while you try not to look too pleased with yourself.)

There is one more sure-fire way to get them clapping, by the way:

9. MAKE IT DIFFICULT FOR THEM TO STOP

This one was invented by the Russian dictator Stalin. He used to get henchmen to stand watch over Communist Party members once he'd finished a speech, to see who would finish clapping first. People were so terrified, they just carried on and on. Some even dropped from exhaustion and were carried out on stretchers. On one occasion, a brave soul – the director of a paper factory – actually sat down after 11 minutes. That night he was arrested and put away for ten years.

★ ★ ★ ★ ★

Clearly then, because of what's at stake – ie power – politicians will do anything to make a good impression. So far we've only listed the tricks of the speaking trade. But it's just as important to get a grip on the Vision Thing – ie how you come across on the box.

Here are some pointers as to how you can do that.

1. LOOK RELAXED

If the audience thinks you're afraid, you're dead. Richard Nixon found this out in a televised debate with John F. Kennedy before the 1960 US presidential elections. Listeners agreed that on the radio, Nixon walked it. But a majority of TV viewers reckoned Kennedy was the winner. That was because Nixon looked shifty, unshaven and – worst of all – sweaty. The camera showed beads of perspiration glistening on his face. JFK, on the other hand, kept cool, looked good, and won the presidency. Moral: being good on TV has nothing to do with winning the argument, but everything to do with having access to a Gillette G2 and a can of antiperspirant.

Most politicians know that being good on TV means being natural, unfussy and informal. But for some, that's not enough: they like to make sure you know it, too. Take Tony Blair. I had to spend a day with him before the 2001 election, for the mighty ITV1 show *Tonight with Trevor McDonald*. The night before, his advisers rang up to ask what we were planning. We told them we thought it would be good if people saw his relaxed and informal side. They obviously agreed with us. The next morning, I met him for the first time on camera and asked him how he was.

'Er… yuh, I'm feeling very relaxed, actually. Very relaxed and informal.'

OK, Tony, we get the picture!

2. LOOK GOOD

Harold Macmillan, who became PM in 1957, was the first to acknowledge the importance of this, albeit reluctantly. He noted that, 'Coming into a TV studio is like entering a 20th-century torture chamber. But we old dogs have to learn new tricks.'

As a result, his dodgy trousers and chippy teeth gave way to pristine suits and a confident, dentally enhanced smile. Mrs Thatcher also had her teeth capped and her hair and clothes overhauled. But Michael Foot, Labour leader in the early 1980s, was a disaster: he used to appear on TV looking like a scarecrow who'd lost a fight with a threshing machine. An all-time low was reached when he turned up at the Cenotaph ceremony on Remembrance Day in a donkey jacket. His defeat at the polls in 1983 was massive – unlike his clothes bill.

3. BE TALL

In every US presidential election since 1945 bar one, the taller man has won. The only exception came in 1976 with Jimmy Carter, who looked up to – but eventually dispatched – Gerald Ford. Women in politics, on the other hand, are allowed to be smaller (Mrs Thatcher was five feet and six inches tall).

4. NEVER FORGET YOU HAVE AN IMAGE

It can be manufactured or genuine, it doesn't matter. But it helps if it's the latter. Tony Blair has a useful character hanging in his wardrobe: Britain's First Rock 'n' Roll

PM. Those shots of him walking into Number 10 with a guitar case and chatting to pop stars at parties do him no harm at all.

Sure, there's a stage-managed element to all this, but there's also an underlying truth there. When yours truly interviewed him in 2001, there was a bit of pre-interview banter before the cameras rolled. I brought up the subject of music to see if he really knew what he was talking about. He did. He went all misty-eyed at the mention of Free, an excellent semi-heavy rock band of the early 1970s, and managed to name – and wax lyrical about – their late guitarist (Paul Kossoff). He also enthusiastically discussed the possibility of a political supergroup, featuring only world leaders. Who, apart from him on guitar, of course, would be in it?

'Uh… Bill, of course. He's into soul and jazz, I mean he's actually a really good musician.'

Aha. Bill Clinton on sax, Tony Blair on guitar. And on vocals?

'The Chinese President.'

No! Really?

'Yes. He sings.'

We even discussed a set list. 'If I Ruled The World' and 'It's My Party' scored highly. But not, alas, 'War! What Is It Good For?' (This was 2001, remember: pre-Iraq.)

William Hague, the then Tory leader, had the opposite problem: the foundations for his chosen image seemed a lot shakier. He was trying to deal with those embarrassing TV pictures of him as a teenager addressing the

Conservative Party conference: bad hair, Dalek voice, zits, etc. So he casually dropped into interviews the fact that he'd once sunk 14 pints of beer in one go. I asked him if he really had. He was adamant that it was true. And what else did he get up to when he was a kid?

'Well, I used to hang around a lot with, um, *girls*, and then sometimes I would go out in a big group, to a dance or something, with *girls*, and then maybe see a show or something with a *girl*...'

OK, William, we get the picture!

5. HAVE HAIR (ON YOUR HEAD BUT NOT YOUR FACE)

Psychological studies show that hair = trustworthiness. There's actually been some proper academic research on this and it was pretty conclusive. A 1990 study in the USA looked at the proportion of baldies in elected office. Out of 522, only 31 were chrome domes. If the baldies had been proportionately represented, however, there should have been 118 of them.

Some argue that lack of hair contributed to William Hague losing the election in 2001. He had so little up top that if you'd put him in a nappy he'd have looked like a baby. He disagreed, though. One interviewer – me, in fact – asked him: 'If you had a full head of hair, and were as handsome as Tony Blair, do you think you'd have a better chance of winning?'

'Er... no.'

Hair on the face, on the other hand, is an electoral

liability. The last PM to risk a moustache was Harold Macmillan in 1963, and the last one to sport a beard was Lloyd George, around the time of WWI. This was not lost on Barbara Follett, Labour's groomer-in-chief before the election of 1997. She ordered a cull on all types of facial fungus. Before long, the party was pretty much 'tache free. Those whose noses ceased to be underlined included big cheeses such as Peter Mandelson, Stephen Byers, Geoff Hoon and Alastair Darling.

These aren't hard-and-fast rules, obviously. You don't have to be a slick, well-groomed shop window dummy. You can always play the 'I'm one of the people' card, and go for the greasy hair, belly and Hush Puppies look, like Kenneth Clarke of the Conservatives. It could have worked, and it still might. Opinion polls show he'd be a hugely popular leader of the Tories. Popular with the public, that is. Unfortunately for the Tories, though, it's not the public who decide their leader, but the Party. So in 2001 they went for Iain Duncan Smith. The headline in the *Mirror* the next day read: 'Tories Choose Unelectable Baldy Number 2'.

So this is what it comes down to: after 800 years of democracy, two world wars, and millions of lives lost, it all rests on whether X or Y comes over better on the telly. But that's not such a terrible thing. After all, what else do we have to go on? It's the same with anyone who's trying to sell you something, be it a used Peugeot or a political policy. In the end, the success of the sale depends on how we react to the person doing the selling.

It's a good 'what if' game to try and work out how different British history would be if TV had been around earlier. Perhaps Winston Churchill would never have become Prime Minister. He tried giving a speech on TV only once, but hated the experience, dismissing it as a 'tuppeny ha'penny Punch and Judy show'. But then he did look like a bulldog chewing a wasp. And even he – the greatest Brit of all – couldn't have foreseen how powerful the 'tuppeny ha'penny' show would become, once Richard had replaced Punch.

In conclusion, then: if you are a balding, ginger gnome called Robin Cook, make sure you have a Plan B, or hope that they ban TV. You don't have to be tall, handsome, charming, relaxed, well dressed and have a full head of hair to be PM... but it sure helps.

CHAPTER FIVE

Are all
Politicians
Liars?

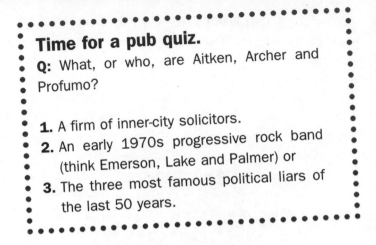

Time for a pub quiz.

Q: What, or who, are Aitken, Archer and Profumo?

1. A firm of inner-city solicitors.
2. An early 1970s progressive rock band (think Emerson, Lake and Palmer) or
3. The three most famous political liars of the last 50 years.

If you picked 3 – and I can't afford a MORI poll on this one, but I'm confident most of you did – then congratulations. You are not only right, but you have, effectively, answered the question posed in the title of this chapter. Because politicians aren't all liars.

It is very rare indeed for them to tell an outright, bare-faced, 24-carat lie – ie something they know is completely untrue. It's not worth it, as they will almost certainly be found out. That's why the names Aitken, Archer and Profumo are so well known. They are the only recent politicians of any note whom we know have told a proper, shameless porky. Politicians who tell genuine 100 per cent lies are very much in the minority. Nevertheless, an awful lot of people take the 'They're bleeding liars, the lot of them' line. This is fashionable I know, but rather sad: it shows how cynical and disillusioned we've all become. We shouldn't judge the majority by the actions of a tiny minority. Mind you, it's not as if the majority are 100 per cent squeaky clean either...

But before we get into that, we need to sort out what real lying involves. Will Messrs Aitken, Archer and Profumo please come to the witness stand.

In 1963, the Conservative Minister of State for War, John Profumo, began bonking a hooker called Christine Keeler. Unfortunately for him, a Russian naval attaché was drinking at the same well, so to speak. This was during the Cold War, and the Russians were our enemies. Tongues began to wag. Profumo tried to stop them by telling the House of Commons that, 'There was no impropriety whatsoever in my relationship with Miss Keeler.' That was a big fib. Profumo was found out, resigned and went on to do years of charity work in London's East End.

The lie that nailed Jeffrey Archer centred on a libel trial in 1987. It was alleged that he'd visited a hooker. He denied it, and came up with an alibi for the night in question and a witness. That helped win him the case. But 14 years later his witness decided to tell the truth, alarmed at the prospect of Archer becoming Mayor of London. The witness revealed that Archer had asked him to lie on his behalf. Archer was found guilty of what the judge called, 'One of the worst cases of perjury I have ever come across'. Archer ended up in the slammer.

Jonathan Aitken, like Archer and Profumo, was a

senior Tory. Aitken had been accused in the press of acting dodgily while he was the Minister of Defence Procurement. It was claimed he'd accepted hospitality from the Saudis when he shouldn't have. He denied the charge, and announced he was going to, 'Cut out the cancer of bent and twisted journalism ... with the simple sword of truth.' Strangely, he attempted to do this by lying. He said that his wife had paid a bill at the Ritz Hotel in Paris when, at the time, she was actually in Switzerland. It turned out that the Saudis had paid it. Aitken was found guilty of perjury and attempting to obstruct the course of justice and was given 18 months.

These cases show why it's so rare for politicians to tell outright lies: sooner or later there's a good chance they'll get caught. For example, it's pointless an MP claiming he never said 'We will abolish VAT', when he knows that there is bound to be a tape, transcript or TV programme somewhere of him saying just that.

So, most MPs, on the whole, don't lie. What they do do, however, is mislead us. To use an old cliché, they are economical with the truth. They give us a false impression. They dissemble. They obfuscate. Here's a quick guide as to how.

1. CLEVER WORDING

'I did not authorise the leaking of the name of David Kelly.'

This is what Tony Blair said after weapons expert

Dr Kelly killed himself in the aftermath of the Iraq War. Poor old Dr Kelly had apparently been unable to cope after being unmasked as the source of a highly controversial story. It revolved around the government's dossier on Iraq's weapons of mass destruction. Had it had been 'sexed up', to increase public and parliamentary support for the war?

This was an ingenious statement by Blair. Have a look at it again. It manages to be technically true, while at the same time giving a highly misleading impression. Yes, it was true that Mr Blair didn't personally rubber-stamp the leaking of Dr Kelly's name. But he was ultimately responsible for it. He allowed it to happen. He was in charge of the process that, inevitably, led to Dr Kelly's name coming out: his officials had nudged, hinted and winked at reporters until they came up with Dr Kelly's name, and then they confirmed it. Tony Blair used to be a barrister, by the way.

But don't think this kind of thing only started when New Labour got into power. Politicians of all hues have been at it for years.

In 1989, former Irish Premier Charles Haughey said of coalition governments: 'They go against every fibre of my being.' Weeks later – surprise, surprise – Mr Haughey led his party into a coalition. His spokesman denied he'd lied, however, arguing: 'Charlie never said he'd *never* lead his party into a coalition, just that he was uncomfortable with the idea in theory. Listen to what he *actually* said, not what you *think* he was implying.'

2. NON-DENIAL DENIAL

This is something that sounds like a denial, but isn't. The phrase was coined by top American hacks Bob Woodward and Carl Bernstein during the Watergate scandal of the early 1970s. A classic example of this came when Michael Heseltine was asked if he would ever challenge Mrs Thatcher for leadership of the Conservative Party. He said he couldn't conceive of a situation in which he would do that. But then – what do you know – he challenged Mrs T for the leadership. He was asked why. A situation had arisen, he said, which he hadn't previously conceived would occur. This is the 'It was technically true – at the time, anyway' defence.

3. THEY CONVINCE THEMSELVES IT'S TRUE, THEREFORE IT MUST BE

Accused of having sex with an intern, President Clinton announced: 'I did not have sexual relations with that woman.' The President had actually been given blow jobs by the woman in question, Monica Lewinsky. So, just as she had, presumably, he must have been swallowing hard when he came up with that line. He had managed to make himself believe he was telling the truth, by convincing himself that sexual relations didn't include oral sex. It was about as dishonest as you can get without actually telling a 24-carat lie. Bill Clinton used to be a lawyer, by the way.

Also in this category come Tony Blair's many statements that start with the words 'I simply say to you...' or 'I passionately believe...' He passionately believed, for example, that there were weapons of mass destruction in Iraq. Later on, of course, it was shown that this was almost certainly not the case. But what *was* true, was that Mr Blair passionately believed it. So in that sense, it wasn't dishonest at all. This tactic is a great one for politicians, as it enables them to say virtually anything and get away with it – eg 'I passionately believe black is white.'

4. REFUSE TO ANSWER THE QUESTION

A classic, this. Turn on the TV or radio at any time and you'll hear a politician being asked about X, but talking about Y. This isn't dishonest in itself, of course, but it is a very useful indicator of what's coming. It's the political equivalent of a road sign that reads 'Danger – Dishonesty Ahead'.

5. PRESENTATIONAL TECHNIQUES, AKA SPIN

You didn't think I could get through a chapter on lying without mentioning the 'S' word, did you? The media have become increasingly obsessed with this topic since New Labour got into power in 1997. But again, what New Labour have done isn't new. They are simply trying, like countless other governments, to present their achievements – and failings – in the best possible light. What *is* new, however, is the professionalism, efficiency and obsessiveness with which they've pursued their aims. That is why the light they have chosen to shine on their achievements has sometimes been a distorting one.

Take the following statement by Chancellor Gordon Brown, in 1999:

'Over the coming three years, I am announcing an increase in health service funding of £21 billion.'

Those words got him loads of cheers in the House of Commons and, far more importantly, bucketfuls of valuable headlines. After all, £21 billion was an unbelievable amount of money. And that was the problem. It *was* an unbelievable amount of money. Spending was actually going to increase from £45 billion a year to £55 billion a year in the period of time he referred to. So the *actual* increase in spending was the difference between £45 billion and £55 billion: ie only £10 billion.

So where on earth did his figure of £21 billion come from? Pay attention: we are going to have a very quick, but revealing, lesson in political maths.

In year 1, health spending was £45 billion.

In year 2, it would be £49 billion: an increase of £4 billion on year 1.

In year 3, it would be £52 billion: an increase of £7 billion on year 1.

In year 4, it would be £55 billion: an increase of £10 billion on year 1.

Now, add together each of those increases in spending, *compared to year 1*, and what do you get: £4 billion + £7 billion + £10 billion. Why, that's £21 billion!

Because they kept going back to year 1 to work out the increase in spending, instead of the previous year, they were able to come up with a much more impressive figure. They justified this by calling it *total* additional expenditure. Others call it good, old-fashioned double counting.

I interviewed Labour's former chairman Charles Clarke about this, for *Tonight with Trevor McDonald*, in 1999. My editor, Jeff Anderson, had decided to make a programme about what was going on called *The Truth Test*. 'Aren't you double counting?' I asked. He accused me of being deliberately dense.

One man who knows all about these ruses is John Humphrys, who has been a presenter on Radio 4's *Today* programme for nearly twenty years. He has grilled more politicians than I have sausages. He also lives 200 yards from me. Although nearly in the bus pass years, he's whippet thin and crackles with nervous energy, like he's just glugged three pints of very strong coffee. Unlike some, he doesn't think it's the worst thing in the world that politicians lie or dissemble, or get economical with the truth, or whatever you want to call it. We all do it, he says, it's part of our nature. 'I mean, if I go to someone's for dinner and she says, "What did you think of that, John?" I might want to say, "Actually, it was fucking disgusting, I only ate it because I haven't eaten for three days and I'm going to be sick right now"… but I don't say that, none of us do, because we don't want to hurt their feelings, so we say, "Mmm, yes, it was lovely, thanks." And that's the point – lying, sometimes, isn't morally wrong. I mean, in the Second World War, if Churchill had told us the truth, all the time, it would have been disastrous for morale, wouldn't it?'

If you want an example of what happens when a politician tells the truth and nothing but, says Humphrys, look at what happened to Enoch Powell. The late Conservative MP for Wolverhampton South-West made a famous speech in 1968 warning of the problems of mass immigration, and predicted that it would result in 'rivers of blood'. His career never recovered. Ironically, many of his predictions turned out to be correct. But that didn't matter. He had made the mistake of being too honest, and telling the truth about how he felt.

The problem, according to Humphrys, is that politics, by its very nature, *encourages* dishonesty. Politics is about getting, and keeping, power. But you can't do that by always being 100 per cent truthful. If you were, you'd sometimes have to admit you'd got it wrong, big time. Or that the other lot were actually right about something. Or that they did, if truth be told, have some very good policies, which would be great for the country. But if you did that, your opponents would make hay, and you'd be out of power in a jiffy. And since you want power more than anything in the world – so you can carry on, as you see it, doing great things for your country – you will do anything to keep it. And if that requires dishonesty, so be it.

Rather than throw our hands up in horror at such

dishonesties, says Humphrys, maybe we should just accept them, and make sure we're better at spotting them. We can do this by being as well informed as possible. Then, if we decide politicians have been too dishonest, for too long, we can give them the ultimate punishment: kick them out.

And maybe we should learn to love them a little bit more, too. Humphrys thinks so, anyway: 'It's a terrible, corny thing to say, but most politicians are actually fundamentally decent. In fact a lot of them are, in many ways, better than the rest of us, because they've got off their arses and said, "What can I do? How can I make the world a better place?" And that's a good thing.'

Hmm. Perhaps we should be saving our bile for journalists, Premiership soccer players and those people with green bibs and clipboards who stop you in the street and say they're collecting for charity.

Having said that, says Humphrys, there are one or two politicians who do actually tell outrageous, copper-bottomed lies: they say something is true when they know full well it isn't.

'How do you know?' I asked.

'Because they've told me.'

'Who?'

'What, you want names?'

'God yes!' I had to switch off my tape recorder. He then told me the name of a famous female politician who has achieved high office and is famed for her integrity.

'She's told me she lies. She's quite open about it. And she doesn't care.'

I'd love to tell you who he was referring to, but I can't: I promised I wouldn't. What's more, I don't want to get sued for 10 million quid. And I cannot tell a lie, of course. Integrity, after all, is very important. In fact, I'm prepared to pay a lot of money for it.

CHAPTER SIX

Who Really Runs Britain: Where the Power is and isn't

Apparently, there aren't that many powerful people in Britain. As in *really* powerful. In fact, according to one person, there are 'only 17 people who count. And to say I am intimate with every one of them is the understatement of the century.'

Those words were spoken by Derek Draper, who was something called 'a New Labour whizz kid'. When he came up with that statement, he found himself splashed all over the national newspapers. Derek's nickname was Dolly, so the scandal was known as 'Dollygate'. With a line like that to his name, I just had to interview him for this chapter.

Dolly was one of those 'government insiders' you read about in newspaper articles. He was also a commercial lobbyist. This entails sucking up to, and trying to influence, those in power. For a fat fee, of course. Fortunately, James (TV producer with impeccable contacts helping me with this book) is a good mate of his. Which is why I find myself sitting outside an expensive café in St John's Wood, London, waiting to meet him.

Things have changed a lot since Dolly said those words. In fact to say he is now *no longer* intimate with the 17 people who count would be the understatement of the century. Shortly after Dollygate (aka 'Lobbygate') he lost his job, his million-pound house and one or two of his marbles. Along the way he got a job as a presenter on a radio station but got sacked after informing the listeners live on air that he was in a bath in Amsterdam in the company of two hookers. Soon after that he had a nervous breakdown and went to America to train as a therapist. Now, six years after Dollygate, he's back and ready to talk.

Except he isn't. At least, not in the way I am hoping. After six therapy-drenched years, his mind is so full of therapy speak he finds it hard to give a straight answer to even the simplest of questions. After my initial greeting – 'Well, hello, Dolly' – it was downhill all the way.

Me: 'So. Commercial lobbyists. How exactly do they work?'

Dolly: 'Aha. It depends what you mean by "work".'

Me: 'Well, they're quite powerful, aren't they? I mean, they have some influence?'

Dolly: 'Aha. It depends what you mean by "influence".'

Me: 'Er… well, they can make things happen, can't they?'

Dolly: 'Aha. It depends what you mean by "making things happen".'

And so on.

Oh dear. I am six years too late. In 1998, Dolly was a front-page story waiting to happen. Quotes poured out of him. Now I can't get him to give me a single useful answer. But he's still a good person to start this chapter with. When he said that stuff about 17 people, he was (albeit unintentionally) making a very important point. Real power in this country – ie the ability to change people's lives – is vested in a relatively tiny number of very important people, many of whom we wouldn't recognise if they bumped into us on the street.

I'm not going to try and name them all, though. That would date this book far too quickly. I'll do it by profession instead. Purely by coincidence, there are – as Derek Draper might say – only 17 categories that count. And I'm intimate with none of them. Right, let's start at the bottom.

1. MEMBERS OF PARLIAMENT

Your average MP has less power than a traffic warden. Many spend their entire parliamentary careers as no more than lobby fodder, ie bodies that can be herded in to the right place at the right time when their party needs them to vote. In this respect, they might as well be dogs on leads. Fortunately for their parties – and their own self-respect – many MPs are drongos, and so don't realise what a sad and largely powerless existence theirs is.

Matthew Parris was an MP for seven years, and was a House of Commons rarity on three counts: intelligent, perceptive about himself and his job, and openly gay. James the impeccably-contacted TV producer, keen to make amends after my fruitless lunch with Derek Draper, fixed up a meeting for me. Matthew is now a newspaper columnist and owns a riverside flat in East London. If you fell off his balcony, you'd land in the Thames. As the dirty old river kept rolling, rolling into the night, I asked him about MPs. How powerless are they?

'Very. It can be quite crushing. When you first get to Westminster, you think you can change the world. You can't.'

If you're an ambitious MP, or want to be one, the stats are depressing. There are around 660 at any one time. But of those, says Matthew only 15, max, will get to be cabinet ministers. There's more chance of Norwich City winning the Premiership than your average MP getting their hands on the steering wheel of power.

What you *can* do though, says Matthew, is make the Government Bus swerve a bit or get the drivers to brake suddenly. It's called being a maverick. If you're lucky you might be able to make a career out of it. This means being a professional pain in the arse to your party, and speaking out publicly when you think they've got it wrong. If you choose this route, you'll end up with plenty of headlines and your integrity intact, but no power. You have committed the cardinal sin of being disloyal and so your party will never promote you. But then, given the Norwich City statistic, you might not care anyway. MPs who have been in this category have included Tam Dalyell and Dennis Skinner. Currently playing the maverick card is a Labour MP called Steven Pound.

I don't want to be defeatist: if you're extremely bright, lucky and patient, you might get to map read for the person who's driving the Government Bus. But then again, if you're bright, lucky and patient, why choose politics in the first place? The hours are appalling and the pay is rubbish: a backbencher earns about 60k a year. At the risk of sounding like Marie Antoinette, that's peanuts for a would-be high flyer. I know dimwits in the City who earn ten times that.

Yes, I know: it's not about money. It's about attracting people who want to do something for their country, people who want to give something back. But if we want the best possible government, then we want the best possible people governing us. And as a general rule, the better the money, the better the people.

And, yes, I also know that the expenses are good. But despite what the papers say, 99 per cent of expense claims are not a source of free money for MPs. If you're representing a 100,000 people at Westminster and you live 250 miles away, it's only fair, surely, that you should be reimbursed for the costs of trying to do your job properly. And even if you take expenses into account, MPs still earn peanuts – compared to high-flyers in the City, anyway.

I have an idea for improving the calibre of MPs, I told Matthew. Why not get rid of 600 of them, and pay the 60 that remain ten times more? That way, you'd get a better standard of politician, and their wages wouldn't be an issue.

'They'd be more capable, but they wouldn't be very representative of the country as a whole. You'd just get a very narrow range of people, a load of career politicians.'

Part of the problem, he says, is that it's frowned upon for politicians to have parallel careers. Which means that MPs with proper jobs and experience of real life are as common as veal burgers at a vegetarian barbie. There are few practising doctors, dentists or teachers in the House of Commons: just a lot of frustrated, impotent time servers.

Out of each batch of 660 MPs, says Matthew, around

20–30 are seriously bright, 500 or so are dull, and about 100 heroically useless. One or two are mad. Literally, barking: he remembers one bloke who used to get on his knees in the House of Commons bar, yapping like a dog and biting women's ankles. But he thinks it's no bad thing that many MPs are drongos. It suits the system, he says.

'People usually make two complaints. That MPs don't have any power, and that they're drongos. But if they're drongos, it's just as well that they've got no power. And if they're never going to get any power, it's also just as well they're drongos, as they never realise what a sad job they've got.'

Then again, let's not be cynical. You can have some effect as an MP. Matthew did. In the mid-1980s, he got the Sexual Offences Bill changed, so prostitutes no longer went to prison. It might not be a big deal to you, but it changed lives. It also gave Matthew a great amount of satisfaction. Did he change the country, or influence the big issues of the day? No. He came nowhere near. But then very few ever do. As he puts it: 'The cockpit of a super-sophisticated jet airline – which is what a modern nation is – is really a very small place, so it's not surprising that not many people fit into it.'

If you're really lucky, you might do the political equivalent of winning the lottery and get your own Private Member's Bill through Parliament. This, in effect, is like inventing your very own private law. One of the most famous of these was David Steel's bill in

1967, which made abortion legal. But again, the odds aren't good. An MP who tries to get a Private Member's Bill on the statute book usually ends up like a rubbish boxer who's taken a shot at the title, ie splattered all over the canvas by the end of round one. Only around 12 Private Member's Bills a year (out of several hundred) make it through, triumphantly, to the final bell, arms aloft. So let us move on.

2. THE QUEEN

Not nearly as powerful as her medieval predecessors, but there are consolations – her private income of around £7 million a year being one. Her role is largely symbolic: she represents Britain abroad, signs treaties, puts in appearances for things like Remembrance Sunday and opens Parliament. She does have some important political privileges, though – according to the bloke who wrote the ultimate text book on this, the 19th-century constitutional expert Walter Bagehot, the Queen has: 'The right to be consulted, the right to encourage, the right to warn.'

She also gets to meet whoever is PM, practically every week, for a debrief. Unfortunately we never get to find out exactly what goes on at these meetings, but it's said that the last time the Queen gave the PM anything like a dig in the ribs was in the 1980s, when she warned Mrs Thatcher that her economic policies were causing problems in Scotland. She is currently said to be all steamed up over global warming which, presumably, will only make it worse.

There is one situation in which the Queen could really come into her own, and that's if there is a general election that produces a neck-and-neck result. In such a case, the Queen has the right to choose the Prime Minister. This nearly happened in February 1974, when Labour won – ie got the most seats – but failed to win an overall parliamentary majority. For a brief spell, the Conservatives considered a power-sharing deal with the Liberals. If they had done so, the Queen would have had to choose between Mr Wilson (Labour) and Mr Heath (Conservative), which would have been fun. But it never came to that. Instead, the country went back to the polls a few months later and gave Mr Wilson something decent to play with, ie an overall majority of seats.

3. TRADE UNIONS

If this book had been written a few decades ago, the unions would have had an entire chapter to themselves. Once upon a time they had so much political muscle that their leader was able to slug it out in the ring, eyeball to eyeball, with the Prime Minister no less, and come out on top. That's actually what happened in 1969. In the red corner was the leader of the Trades Union Congress (TUC), Hugh Scanlon. And in the – er – other red corner was the Labour PM, Harold Wilson, who wanted to limit the unions' ability to strike. He famously told Scanlon, 'Get your tanks off my lawn, Hughie.'

But Hughie kept them right there and in the end it was Wilson who retreated. One year later there was an election and the country kicked Wilson out. Hughie's tanks stayed firmly put for ten more years.

The unions' power stemmed from three things:

1. Their sheer numbers. In the late 1960s, the TUC had 13 million members. This was partly due to something called the 'closed shop', which meant that pretty much anyone who got a job had to join a union, or they wouldn't be employed.

2. The ease with which they could strike. In the 1970s they weren't legally obliged to hold a vote before a strike. If your union representative said, 'Right lads: out!' – and he did, frequently – then that was it. You effectively had no choice. Sure, there were some legal procedures to follow before strikes could be called – but some shop stewards, particularly in the engineering industry, couldn't give a monkey's about them. So they simply called strikes – unofficial ones, but no less damaging for that – pretty much when they felt like it. It didn't quite get to the stage where they walked out over the quality of the tea bags in the staff canteen, but some of the stoppages were over piddly points of principle. By 1979, and the so-called Winter of Discontent, things were so out of control that 29 million working days were lost to strikes.

3. They were politically joined at the hip to the Labour Party. So much so that you still can't be a Labour MP unless you're a member of a union. Labour and the unions are close because they have a shared history and common political objectives. (Or at least they did until Tony Blair came along.) And many – but not all – unions give financial support to the party as well, via something called the levy.

The unions were important enough to be, arguably, the decisive factor in all four general elections in the 1970s. In 1974, for example, the Tories based their entire campaign on the issue. When they came up with their slogan 'Who Governs Britain?', everyone knew who they were referring to.

But it's oversimplistic, even by this book's standards, to paint the unions as strike-hungry bad guys. They did – and still do – an essential and honourable job, stopping workers from being exploited by their bosses. If it weren't for unions, companies would still be getting kids to work more than 60 hours a week for less than 50p a day. (As, indeed, they still do in the TV industry, funnily enough...)

But in the 1980s, things changed. Union-basher supreme Mrs Thatcher came along. She reckoned that the unions had grown lazy, complacent and corrupt and were having the same effect on British businesses as a sack of spuds on the back of a marathon runner. To be fair, the unions hadn't caused many of the problems of that time:

there had been an economic crisis. But they were making a bad situation worse. In the newspaper industry, for example, some employers had to pay (extremely handsomely) up to 18 men to operate just one printing press. In most countries around the world the same job was being done by six men or fewer. Employers knew the deal, though: if anyone even dared to suggest that, um, there might be the teensiest bit of overmanning going on, the unions would threaten a full-scale strike. This led one commentator (Bernard Levin) to say that British newspapers were produced '...in conditions which combined a protection racket with a lunatic asylum.'

Mrs Thatcher sprang into action. Bosh! In 1980, she passed a law limiting union power. Their tank drivers, for the first time in years, had to find reverse gear. Then, in 1982, bosh! Another law. New acts curbing union power were introduced repeatedly – in 1984, 1988, 1990 and 1993. By the time the last one hit the statute book the closed shop had been outlawed, the right to strike had been severely curtailed, and the once-mighty union tanks were lying idle and useless in the TUC depot.

They couldn't even rely on their old chums in the Labour Party to bail them out. In the 1980s, the then Labour leader Neil Kinnock began putting clear blue water between the two organisations. By the time Tony Blair had bunged 'New' in front of 'Labour', there was a small lake between them.

As a result, union membership shrank. In the late 1970s, remember, the unions had 13 million members.

By 2000, that number had halved. And although they can still strike, today it's more of a last resort than an instinctive reaction. That's why the number of days lost to industrial action has fallen, staggeringly, by more than 95 per cent since that discontented winter.

The unions do still have power in one very important area, though. In return for the financial support they give the Labour Party, they get, according to one of their fact sheets, 'a direct input into policy making'. This is more exciting than it sounds. If you make policies – or help to – then you have, potentially, the power to change people's lives. But this direct input is only relevant when the Labour Party is governing us. And there's an awful lot of other people, and organisations, who have a direct input into policy making.

Experts in these matters, ie Oxbridge professors of politics, reckon the unions are now at a low point and that this is A Bad Thing. A strong, healthy democracy, they say, needs a strong union movement to challenge politicians and stop them getting too powerful. But it's hard to see how the union tanks can roll again like they used to given that their engines, gearboxes and petrol supply were all but obliterated by Mrs Thatcher.

4. THE HOUSE OF LORDS

The main job of the House of Lords is to keep an eye on the House of Commons and make sure it doesn't become too powerful. This is what is meant by 'a system of checks and balances': the Lords act as a check on the

91

Commons. They do this by twiddling with House of Commons bills and occasionally saying, 'No, hold on a minute, you can't do that.'

In theory, the Lords should now be very good at amending and improving legislation, as a lot of them are experts in their fields – which is more than you can say for many MPs. Lord (Melvin) Bragg, for example, is well handy when it comes to discussing new laws on the Arts and TV, as he's made a career out of both.

The House of Lords, which currently has 677 members, is mainly populated by these experts. They're called life peers. Before life peers were invented in 1958 the place was full of hereditary peers, ie people who had inherited their title. Because the House of Lords was full of these overprivileged, thick coffin-dodgers (as some saw them), it was one of the most undemocratic places in the world. That's why the current government reformed it. Hereditary peers are now in the minority, and on the way out: only about 90 are left.

The Lords don't use their power to say, 'No, hold on a minute' to a Bill too often. But their power to delay can be used to great effect. The last time it really mattered was when something called the Criminal Justice (Mode Of Trial) Bill was in front of them in 2000. They didn't like the fact that it limited a person's right to be tried by a jury. So they got awkward. It worked. In the end, the Home Secretary, David Blunkett, gave up on the idea altogether.

The Lords are well aware, however, that if they do this

too often, they'll cause trouble for themselves. So they tend to use their powers sparingly. They know that in the event of a head-to-head fight, there can only be one winner. They found this out the hard way, in 1909.

That was the year it all went pear-shaped for their Lordships. Before then they could, and occasionally did, reject House of Commons bills outright. But in 1909 they tried to stop the government's budget becoming law. The PM, David Lloyd George, got mad and threatened to cut off their political balls, so they backed down. To ensure this would never happen again, the Parliament Act was passed in 1911. This meant the Lords could only ever delay bills, not reject them. That turned them from being big, dangerous Dobermans with the power to kill, into what they are today: something akin to poodles. But poodles that still occasionally bite. Most of the time, though, they simply yap. In fact, yapping is their speciality. They're great at reminiscing, advising and analysing. But it's all a bit past tense: almost everybody there *has been* somebody, once. Rather fewer are anybody much, now. At a crash – involving cars, software or the city – the cry, 'Let me through, I'm from the House of Lords!' is unlikely to clear the way.

5. CIVIL SERVANTS

Do you know what a top civil servant looks like? No, I don't either. Yet they are among the most powerful people in the land. They might go about their business quietly, unnoticed by the rest of us, but then again, as Confucius might have said, he who swims with his fin submerged eats the heartiest breakfast.

Ministers make key decisions that affect us all, but it's civil servants who provide the all-important advice on which those decisions are based. Civil servants aren't supposed to run the country, but they know exactly *how* it's run, which can sometimes amount to the same thing. They are the unelected bureaucrats who know better than anyone how the system works. They're sometimes called 'mandarins'. This is what the Chinese – who had the first-ever civil service, more than 2000 years ago – called their officials. There are about 500,000 civil servants in the UK at the moment, but for the purposes of this chapter, there are only a few dozen we need to worry about: the ones that advise ministers.

The most powerful civil servants are called, somewhat misleadingly, 'secretaries'. But this lot don't do dictation. The ones with the real clout are the Permanent Secretaries. Each government department – ie Agriculture, Education, Industry and so on – will have at least one Permanent Secretary, as well as gaggle of Second Permanent Secretaries.

There's a clue as to why Permanent Secretaries are so powerful. It's in the title. Elected governments may come and go, but civil servants generally stay put. So it's not surprising, given their greater experience, that they sometimes outmanoeuvre ministers, especially new ones. The following comparison may help to explain why.

The civil service has been likened to a Rolls-Royce: under the bonnet is a mass of immensely complicated sprockets, plugs and fuses. But they all fit together so smoothly that even when the engine is running, all you can hear is the ticking of the clock. When new ministers arrive in big government departments, some of them don't even know where the petrol cap is. So they often end up being utterly dependent on their senior civil servants.

Top civil servants also write, and come up with the ideas for, an enormous number of the laws that get passed by Parliament every year. As much as 80 per cent of new legislation is simply bog-standard stuff that reflects the everyday demands of running a country. We're talking about things such as the Judicial Pensions Act and The Road Traffic (New Drivers) Act. The boring but necessary stuff.

The favourite tool of top civil servants is called a 'submission'. They love 'em. Some write more submissions than traffic wardens issue parking tickets. They are (usually) extremely well-written documents of about three to four pages, which identify problems and issues and suggest solutions. Suitable subjects include closures of canning factories in Grimsby, football hooliganism and flooding in low-lying coastal towns – in other words, anything and everything.

Your clever, experienced senior civil servant will write their submission in a suitably cunning way so that the minister will be drawn to one particular course of action, even though more than one has been offered. This process was expertly described by yet another bald bloke with glasses – Gerald Kaufman, a former Labour minister who wrote a book called *How To Be A Minister*. He may have penned it a long time ago (1980) but it's as relevant now as it's ever been: the moment someone becomes a minister, they usually go to bed with Gerald. As it were.

Gerald Kaufman says the power that top civil servants have is often negative. If they don't agree with a certain course of action, they may be able to block it, slow it down, or have it dropped altogether. This can be done in a number of ways. Here's a favourite one. Say a Parliamentary Private Secretary (PPS) – let's call him Sir Digby Cole-Mackintosh – has handed in one of his beloved submissions, but the minister has ignored all his solutions and come up with one of his own. (In the old days the civil service was dominated by Old Etonian, double-barrelled Oxbridge types like Sir Digby. Less so now. But women and ethnic minorities are still massively underrepresented.)

Sir Digby, a canny operator, feels the minister is about to drive the Whitehall Rolls-Royce into a bollard. He picks up the phone and dials his opposite number at the Treasury, Sir Gordon. The Treasury is the most important Whitehall department of all, as it controls the finances. Without the support of the Treasury, the minister hasn't a hope of getting what he wants. Sir Digby tells Sir Gordon what a plonker the minister is. Sir Gordon tells

Sir Digby not to worry. The next day the minister gets a note from the Treasury saying: 'Sorry: no can do, pal.' The minister is shafted. Yes, I know: it sounds like a thinly disguised scene from *Yes, Minister*. But according to Gerald, and others who've been there and done that, this is exactly how it works.

Civil servants should be utterly neutral. They must serve the best interests of their country, not whichever government happens to be in power. Traditionally, they're supposed to ask themselves only one question when a minister wants something. Not 'Do I agree?', but 'Can it be done?' However, that much-valued impartiality went by the board a fair bit after New Labour came to power in 1997. The party started bringing in highly paid, professional special advisers like Alastair Campbell (you didn't think I could write a book about politics without mentioning him, did you?).

Now Alastair Campbell is – or rather was – technically speaking, a civil servant. But many in the old school feel he tarnished the good name of the civil service by shamelessly serving the interests of his political masters. Campbell was about as neutral as a football fan, it is true, but you can't lay the blame for injecting too much politics into the civil service solely at his and Tony Blair's door. Mrs Thatch did much the same thing back in the 1980s, when she injected the civil service with a load of top business types from the City, to help her get things done; she'd grown frustrated by what she saw as fuddy-duddies, opposed to progress.

Conclusions: ministers and politicians will always try and get one over on civil servants, and vice versa. The government of the day may be at the steering wheel, but if it wasn't for the civil service, they wouldn't be able to get the bus out of the garage.

6. FOCUS GROUPS AND BRIGHT YOUNG THINGS

Both of which have power, in that they can create policies. Or at least make a serious contribution to them. The political equivalent to the question 'Mummy, where do babies come from?' is 'Daddy, where do policies come from?' In the case of babies, there are – with one exception, if you believe the Bible – only ever two parents. But with policies there are often several. Especially if they've worked. After all, success, as they say, has many parents. Failure, on the other hand, is an orphan.

Each party has its own way of coming up with new policies. New Labour is particularly fond of focus groups. These usually consist of between 12 and 20 people who are representative of society as a whole – black, white, rich, poor, professional, unemployed etc. They are bunged in a room, given chocolate Hobnobs and tea, and asked loads of questions such as: 'What do you think of this policy on health?' and 'What do you think the government should be spending its money on?' Some people think focus groups are a bad idea. It's not the job of voters to think up policies, they say, that's what politicians are for: it's like the tail wagging the dog. Others argue that a good government should be – to use political cliché No. 1,456 – 'responsive to the needs of its people'.

Bright young things are often called 'special advisers'. Practically every minister has one or more, as do most senior members of the opposition parties. The Chancellor, Gordon Brown, for example, had the Two Eds: Ed Milliband and Ed Balls. They followed him everywhere – even into top-level meetings – and were not averse to whispering advice loudly in his ear if the situation demanded it. Mr Brown probably could have got by with just one special adviser, but then two Eds are better than one.

Bright young things will often write speeches for ministers, or pen articles for them. These articles will then appear in the papers looking as if they've been written personally by the minister in question, which they practically never are. I think this is a bit dishonest, but no one else seems to care.

Currently, the Number 10 Policy Unit, which helps the government make up its mind on big issues, is also brim full of special advisers. They also crop up, in alarmingly large numbers, about a year or two before general elections, to help draw up party manifestoes.

Special advisers have been known to get slagged off in the press, as they're not elected, and the worry is that some of them have too much power. But you've got to get advice from somewhere, haven't you? And anyway, they've been around for centuries: think back to King Henry XVIII and his courtiers.

7. QUANGOS

Quangos? Powerful? Yes, some of them are. But before we go into that, let's just establish what they are and what they do.

There are more quangos than there are curry houses in Manchester. Quangos are organisations set up by the government to do some of their donkey-work for them. The word stands for Quasi-Autonomous Non-Governmental Organisations, but it could just as easily be GOODDies: Government Organisations Overseeing Delegated Donkey-work.

Quangos can be big or small. They can employ thousands of people, or be bite-sized advisory bodies that meet once a year. In the 'high and mighty' category, for example, is the Environment Agency, which employs 10,000 people and has around £800 million a year at its disposal. There's also the Human Fertilisation and Embryology Authority (HFEA), which can license or close down clinics, and make life-or-death decisions about things such as cloning and embryo research. The big quangos spend around £20 billion of government money between them. Usually, if a quango is important, an Act of Parliament will be needed to create it.

In the Not Quite As Important category – quaint quangos – you get things like the Apple and Pear Research Council. There are also lots of organisations that might not call themselves quangos, but which have been described as such: for example, local NHS health trusts, OFCOM (Office of Telecommunications – the body that regulates broadcasting) and OFWAT (Office of Water Services, who look after the water industry).

No one knows exactly how many quangos there are: depending on how you define them, there are between 850 and 5,000. In fact there are so many that the current government set up a task force to see if there were too many. Yes, that's right. A quango to investigate quangos.

In theory, quangos are very good things. They are staffed by experts in their fields, and are fairly independent, if that's not a contradiction in terms. That means they can make decisions in the best interests of the public, and not whichever party happens to be in government.

Actually, everyone loves quangos, but for different reasons. Governments are fans, because they reduce the workload. Opposition parties love them because they're a good stick to beat the government with. Common criticisms of quangos include the following: they are unnecessary, and/or a waste of public money, and/or too powerful. Another bugbear is that their members aren't elected, but given the posts simply on a ministerial say-so. Oh, and Scrabble players love them because QUANGO is now an officially approved word. As is QUANGOS. Put either on a triple word score and you'll understand why.

One word of warning: because quangos have had such a bad press, they've tried changing their name to NDPBs (Non-Departmental Public Bodies). The hope was that people wouldn't slag them off as much, as 'NDPB' is much more difficult to say than 'quango'. But don't be fooled. An NDPB is, to all intents and purposes, a quango in disguise.

The current government has promised to get rid of some quangos. But that hasn't happened yet. At the moment, it's a case of quangoing... quangoing... but not quite quangone.

8. NATIONAL PARLIAMENTS AND ASSEMBLIES

When New Labour took over in 1997 they started handing back large chunks of power to places such as Scotland, Wales and Northern Ireland. Thanks to Devolution, Scotland now has its own Parliament (and very expensive Parliament building) and Wales and Northern Ireland each have their own Assembly.

The Scottish Parliament is the most powerful of the three. It has 129 members. It can pass new laws about things such as agriculture, health, education, transport and the environment. Most important of all, it can vary the amount of tax paid by the Scottish people. But some important stuff – like defence and foreign affairs – still rests with the big boys in Westminster. And it's still funded from London. The Scottish Parliament is like a teenager who hasn't left home: it can stay out late, dress how it wants and hang out with who it likes – but the parents – ie Westminster – are the ones who supply the pocket money and are therefore ultimately in charge.

The Welsh Assembly came into being after a referendum of the Welsh people. It was hardly an overwhelming decision, however: only one in four of the total population voted for it. The Welsh Assembly, which has 60 members, is less powerful than its Scottish counterpart. It can only pass secondary legislation. This means it can interpret laws, but it can't come up with new ones. Say, for instance, that Westminster has said there must be a national curriculum in schools. That's the primary legislation. The Welsh Assembly would then be free, under its secondary legislative powers, to decide exactly which subjects should be taught in that curriculum. This, not surprisingly, has led to accusations that the Assembly is no more than a mass debating chamber. Or maybe even a chamber for mass debaters, as Bernard Manning might say.

The Northern Ireland Assembly came into being as a result of the Good Friday Agreement of 10 April 1998. It has 108 members and the power to run most of Northern Ireland's affairs. Indeed, 10 April 1998 was a day memorable not only because it opened a brand new and more peaceful chapter in the region's history, but also because it enabled Tony Blair to come up with the following statement:

'This is not a time for sound bites.' (Pause, for effect.) 'I feel the hand of history on my shoulder.'

Over the next four years, the Assembly passed 27 acts. However, due to events – ie problems over proving whether or not the IRA had actually got rid of its weapons or not – it was suspended in October 2002. By the time you read this it may have been reinstated.

That's the thing with regional assemblies: like busses you can wait 250 years for one, then three come along at once. This number clearly wasn't enough for the Government though, which immediately started making noises about more, for different bits of England: Humberside, the North West, the South West, etc. But in November 2004, the people of the North East showed what they thought of that. They stuck two very big fingers right in front of the Government's face and voted – by a margin of more than four to one – *against* their own regional assembly. They'd clearly done the (very simple) maths and realised that we already have lots of governments (national ones, local ones, etc) and that actually, we might quite like *less* government, not more. As a result, this issue – for the time being at least – has 'dead' stamped all over it.

9. BIG BUSINESS

Some businesses are bigger, richer and more powerful than entire countries. In the year 2000, a list of the 100 largest economies in the world was published. Of that 100, 51 were corporations and only 49 were countries. The oil company Exxon, for example, was the same size, economically, as Chile or Pakistan. Even an oil-rich country such as Nigeria was ranked alongside Daimler-Chrysler and General Electric in terms of wealth. And Phillip Morris, who make fags, are on a par with Tunisia, Slovakia and Guatemala. Imagine where they'd be if we actually smoked.

Big businesses don't run Britain, of course: they don't want to. They just want to become even more wealthy. But if something threatens that, they can get the people who *do* run Britain to help them out. We might pride ourselves on the integrity of our democracy, but money talks in modern Britain as loudly as anywhere else.

So how do big businesses get governments to help them? They use lobbyists. This, you will recall, is where Derek 'Dolly' Draper came in. He was a lobbyist, ie someone who charges you, big time, to put your case, extremely persuasively, to people that matter. Lobbying companies charge anything from between £5,000 and £20,000 a week, and are run by people with the most valuable address books in town.

One of the most successful lobbying companies of recent years has been Lawson, Lucas Mendelsohn (LLM). They had a long list of rich and powerful clients, which included Rupert Murdoch's News International. LLM's job was to make sure their clients stayed rich and powerful. They were good at this because they had previously worked with the most powerful people in Britain, and remained on good terms with them. So who are Lawson, Lucas and Mendelsohn? Neal Lawson advised Tony Blair on campaign strategy. Ben Lucas used to run his political briefings. And Jon Mendelsohn used to organise the pre-PM Blair's contacts with big business.

June 1998. Enter Tesco, stage right. With a small problem. The government are about to put a green tax on parking lots to try and stop people using their cars. Tesco are not in favour of this, as it'll cost them more than £20 million a year. So they pay LLM to put their case for them at the highest level. Hey presto, a short time later, the plans for the tax are – to use LLM's word – 'derailed'. But that's not the end of it. Tesco bung £11 million into the government's Millennium Dome project, and everyone is happy. Apart from the greenie brigade who proposed the parking tax, that is. The government would argue that the two events weren't linked and that they would have eventually dropped plans for the tax anyway. What do you think?

But firms like LLM aren't just about dropping a few well-chosen words in the right ears. They also hang around with people who have access to privileged and potentially valuable information, and they have no qualms about passing it on to clients. In June 1998, for example, Ben Lucas knew, in advance, that Chancellor Gordon Brown was going to announce the creation of a new housing inspectorate. He knew this because he was speaking to the people who were writing the Chancellor's speech. He gave this information to one of his clients, and advised them how to make money from it.

I know all this because a bald American journalist (but without glasses) called Greg Palast wrote about lobbying companies like LLM in an interesting little book called *The Best Democracy Money Can Buy*. It is Greg to whom Derek 'Dolly' Draper made his 'understatement of the century' remark – at the time, Greg was posing as a potential client with lots of money to spend. In his book, Greg metaphorically and repeatedly bangs his chrome dome against the wall over this kind of thing. He thinks it is appalling and undemocratic that it goes on. But in both the examples just given, nobody did anything illegal: not Tesco, not LLM, not the government, not the Chancellor's speech writers and not the people Ben Lucas passed the valuable information on to. It might make you feel uneasy, but this is the way the system works: as the cliché goes, it's not what you know, but who. In fact, arguably, in the case of Tesco and the parking tax, some 'good' came out of it: Tesco made more money for their shareholders and motorists managed to avoid yet another tax on driving.

The Tories did this kind of thing when they were in government too, of course, but back then it was a lot more ham-fisted and sleazy. In the early 1990s, people didn't keep a close eye on lobbying like they do now. It wasn't deals in high places, it was brown envelopes stuffed with cash, in return for questions beings asked in Parliament.

You might not like the way big companies try to curry favour with the government – but then again, why shouldn't they? And why shouldn't people like LLM make money out of advising them how to? After all – and here's another cliché for you – money makes the world go round.

There is one big problem, though. It's potentially

very unfair. What happens, for example, if you're too poor to afford a lobbyist? Greg Palast tells the story of an organisation who were appalled at the prospect of the government disconnecting the gas and electricity supplies of people who couldn't pay their bills. But the organisation didn't have the dosh to pay the LLMs of this world. They tried to reach the people that mattered, but couldn't get anywhere near the front door, let alone the corridors, of power. The gas and electricity companies, meanwhile, hired the very best lobbying firms money could buy. Surprise surprise, the big companies won the day. Some might say: 'Well, it was the right end result, so who cares? If you start letting some people off their gas bills, then everyone will want the same: the big companies won, because they were right.' That may be the case. But was it fair that the people lobbying for the poor never even got to put their case properly in the first place?

Interestingly, even one of the Ls in LLM agrees that it's unfair. I rang Neal Lawson – who will have left the company by the time you read this – and asked him what he thought about the system. He admitted there was a 'fundamental inequality' in the way lobbying works, and that it troubled him. He told me: 'The problem is that the business world and the political world seem to be merging.' But sometimes, he added, poor people can have effective voices raised on their behalf. 'Take the Drop the Debt Campaign – Bob Geldof and Bono, the pop stars, they did very well when they went round persuading world leaders to let up on some of the poorer countries' debts.' Unfortunately, this is the exception, not the rule.

It's not just big businesses who wield power. Disgustingly rich individuals can also, it seems, sometimes get eyebrow-raisingly special treatment just because they're loaded. In fact, there have been several examples of this since the current government came to power. For example, after the steel tycoon Lakshmi Mittal donated £125,000 to the Labour Party, Tony Blair wrote a letter to the President of Romania, urging him to let Mittal open a steel factory there. The PM denied doing anything wrong. He didn't write the letter because Mittal had given money, he said: he would have written it anyway. The fact that Mittal was worth £3.5 billion had nothing to do with it.

Then there was the Bernie Ecclestone affair. The Formula One boss gave £1 million to Labour, who then tried to get the sport exempted from a European tobacco advertising ban. Again, Tony Blair 'denied linkage', as they say. He would like to think, he said, that people knew he was a 'pretty decent kind of guy' and would never behave improperly.

Then there was the case of the controversial Indian billionaire Srichand Hinduja. He pledged £1 million in sponsorship to the Millennium Dome, Labour's pet project. The Northern Ireland Secretary at the time, Peter Mandelson, then personally stepped in to help Mr Hinduja get a British passport. Mandelson claimed he'd done nothing wrong, but after questions were raised about the propriety of his actions he resigned anyway. Crucially, in none of these cases was there a smoking gun, eg a letter saying: 'Please give them a passport. After all, they have given us lots of money.'

But then again, in cases like these, there never is.

10. THE BANK OF ENGLAND

I'm not going into a long, boring economics lesson, don't worry. All you need to know is that the Bank of England is a lot more powerful than it used to be, for one reason. In 1997, within five days of Labour's election win, Gordon Brown, the Chancellor of the Exchequer, gave the Bank the power to set interest rates. Previously, that had been the government's job, hence concern that rates were being fiddled with for the wrong reasons – ie not for the good of the country, but for the benefit of whichever party was in government. Now, however, the Bank of England decides the rate. Or rather its Monetary Policy Committee does. Which is why the Bank now has a massive influence over things like your mortgage, prices in the shops and jobs.

11. THE CABINET

The Cabinet is usually made of up of 22 ministers – it can be as many as 24 – who are appointed by the PM. Its power depends on how much notice the PM wants to take of it. John Major, the Conservative PM from 1992–7, paid his Cabinet a lot of attention. Under

Major, if a simple majority in the Cabinet wanted something, it would happen.

The Cabinet meets regularly, but that doesn't mean much. Tony Blair's meets at least once a week, but he still gets slagged off for ignoring it. Occasionally, on some matters, he will bypass it altogether. This is where the shirtsleeves, chinos and mug of coffee come in. Armed with all three, he will go into something called the Den and say, 'Hi, I'm Tony' to a bunch of young, thrusting, up-and-coming special advisers, known as the Sofa Cabinet. And they will then thrash out what the government's policy should be on X, Y or Z.

Because these Den-type meetings are all very informal, records usually aren't kept. Obviously, this annoys senior civil servants very much, as they like to do things by the book, which means taking a note of everything that is said. Sometimes this lack of note-taking isn't a problem. But sometimes it's a very big one, especially when the subject under discussion is: 'Should we go to war with Iraq and risk thousands of British soldiers getting killed?'

To be fair though, Tony Blair isn't the first PM to behave like this. Harold Wilson, Labour PM in the 1960s, was rumoured to have his own, unofficial, 'Kitchen Cabinet'. Mrs Thatcher did at least listen to what her Cabinet had to say – then she would simply ignore it.

If this sounds undemocratic, tough cheese: there's nothing anyone can do about it, except maybe bleat to the press. That's because the Cabinet doesn't officially exist. There's no law, or written constitution, which says what it is, or what its powers are. It's simply up to the person in charge. Cabinet government is not dead, however: it is merely sleeping. And one day, for better or worse, it will return.

12. MINISTERS

The amount of power ministers have depends on two things: 1) what department they're in charge of and 2) their own personality and ability. It is said the three most powerful positions in government, apart from Prime Minister, are Home Secretary, Chancellor and Foreign Secretary. I'm not too sure about the last one. If the Foreign Secretary had decided, in 2002, that it wasn't such a good idea to go to war with Iraq after all, he would simply have been told to get stuffed. Which in my book doesn't make him very powerful at all.

If ministers want to maximise what power they have, they must, as we've seen, be able to keep the civil service on their side. If they don't they may find themselves verging on the impotent. This happened to Tony Benn in the 1960s, when he was in charge of the Department of Industry. He pissed off the entire department, so they cold-shouldered him. A canny minister, however, will find a way to get round whatever objections senior advisers may have without alienating them.

The following is Gerald Kaufman's example of How To Be A Canny Minister. When he was in government, he tried to get the Treasury to stump up for a new type of airliner. He thought it was a great idea but lots of important civil servants didn't. He got the thumbs down. Many would have left it there, but not Gerry. He persuaded every single member of the Cabinet that he should get his way. They agreed with him. The next time they met, he got their permission to announce it publicly, in Parliament. He did so immediately, before any irate civil servants could object. There could be no going back after that, as it would have embarrassed the government. Game set and match to Gerry, the cunning little fox.

The difference between a good minister and a bad one is massive. If they really know their stuff and can argue passionately but coherently, ministers can take on the biggest gun in town, ie the PM, and win. A bloke called Peter Walker, a minister in Mrs Thatcher's government, once did this. She wanted one course of action – it was a Welsh issue – he, another. He stood firm. She gave in. He lived.

A bad minister, if they're unusually honest, will simply admit it and resign. There are many more incompetent government ministers than you might think, but their shortcomings are usually kept hidden. Not from themselves, though. One senior minister in the current Labour government was being given media training. It wasn't going very well. She broke down in tears, admitting she felt useless and couldn't do her job. There are two ways of looking at this. One is: 'Only a woman could be so self-aware. That alone makes her a better minister than most.' The other is: 'If she's so crap, what's she doing in the job in the first place and why hasn't she resigned?'

Some ministers can be surprisingly vague on important matters of detail. When Norman Fowler was in charge of the Department of Health, the AIDS crisis was a big issue. But Norm had a problem. He knew it could be transmitted by oral sex, but he didn't know what oral sex was. A flunkey had to explain. Norm went pale and quiet. A few seconds later, he said just the one word: 'Blimey.'

13. THE PRESS

If you believe the newspapers, they can win elections. In 1992, for example, the *Sun* took the credit for the Tories' victory, crowing: 'It Was The *Sun* Wot Won It!' This was a reference to the paper's front page on the day of the election itself. Even-handed as ever, it had featured a picture of Labour's Neil Kinnock inside a light bulb, accompanied by the headline: 'If Neil Kinnock Wins Today, Will the Last Person to Leave Britain Please Turn Out the Lights.'

So Woz It The *Sun* Wot Won It? Almost certainly not. John Major won in 1992, experts argue, because Labour was in its so-called 'unelectable' period, and the British public simply didn't trust Kinnock to be their leader, as he was Welsh, and/or ginger, and/or too close to the unions, and/or a windbag. In other words, the *Sun* didn't lead public opinion, it reflected it.

But while the *Sun* may have been less powerful than it liked to think, it was – and still is – hugely influential. And prime ministers know it, as indicated by the excellent story involving former *Sun* editor Kelvin Mackenzie and John Major. After the catastrophic cock-up on economic policy known as Black Wednesday, the former PM called Mackenzie to see what was going to be on the *Sun*'s front page. Mackenzie claims he said, 'Put it this way, Prime Minister. I have a very big bucket of shit and I'm about to throw it all over you.'

Master and servant, anyone?

Tony Blair, on the other hand, seemed to think it may well have been The *Sun* Wot Won It, as he bust a gut getting the paper to support New Labour before the 1997 general election. And he has carried on doing so ever since. Much to the alarm of some observers. This next story – about Tony, Rupert (Murdoch) and Irwin (Stelzer) – shows why there's such concern.

First, though, let's just establish why Rupert Murdoch is a very important person. He owns more papers than anyone else in the UK – the *Sun*, *The Times*, the *Sunday Times* and the *News of the World* – and these are read by up to 20 million different Britons a week. Anyway, in early 2004 Tony Blair suddenly announced that we were going to have a national referendum on Europe. This was very strange, because previously Mr Blair had been dead against it. So what changed his mind? It didn't take long for an explanation to emerge. One of Rupert Murdoch's key right-hand men, the American economist Irwin Stelzer, is very close to Tony Blair; they meet regularly. It transpired that Stelzer had made it clear, during one of their meetings, that unless there was a referendum on

Europe, the four Murdoch papers would not back Labour in a general election. And so, according to commentators, 'a deal was done'. That is why, when Mr Blair announced the referendum, he looked, in the words of one MP: 'Like a hostage making a false confession on TV because there is a hooded man with a gun at his head.'

Is it fair and democratic that an Australian-American can virtually dictate British government policy in certain areas? Not really. But life isn't fair. Mr Blair was, I think, guilty only of practising what is called realpolitik (ie making big decisions for practical reasons, not moral ones). And anyway, he's not the first PM to have courted the press, big time, and he won't be the last. The current Tory Leader of the Opposition, Michael Howard, spends a lot of time trying to impress Mr Murdoch. And it could be a lot worse: in Italy, their president actually owns a huge chunk of the media. Now that's really unhealthy.

Pardon me if I'm stating the obvious (again), but it's worth, I think, saying *why* the media are so hugely important. There are a vast amount of crucial issues out there in the world, but the only way any of us gets access to them is via the media. They shape our opinions on just about everything. Which is why politicians are so obsessed with controlling the way that information is presented. Yes, I am talking about spin doctors, I'm afraid.

Some would say spin doctors deserve a separate heading all of their own. I'm not sure. There was one extremely powerful spin doctor, of course: Alastair Campbell. It's even been said that he had a hand in making big policy decisions. And he was, of course, a central figure in persuading us that it was right to bomb Iraq. But let's not get carried away. He didn't make the decision to go to war himself – Tony Blair (and Parliament) did. And anyway, Alastair Campbell was an exception: no other spin doctor had ever wielded such power. What's more, he is a spin doctor no more. Nowadays, all your average government spin doctor does is try and pull the wool over the media's eyes. The media complain about this, but it's hard to have sympathy with them. It is, after all, their job to *see through* the wool, not bleat about it.

Another example of media power: sometimes they can, effectively, make their own laws. For instance, it was a series of stories in newspapers that led directly to the Dangerous Dogs Act in 1991, and the Sex Offenders Act in 1997. In both cases, the risk to the public – from wild dogs and paedophiles respectively – was tiny. What's more, the risks weren't on the increase. They'd been very small indeed, for many years. So there was actually no need for these Acts. But in both cases the government felt obliged to do something. They simply couldn't ignore the public's concern – which had been whipped up by the media.

The press are like the House of Lords: they'll rarely make the Government Bus do a complete U-turn, but they'll sometimes force it to take another route, so it ends up in a slightly different place. This looked as if it might be happening in late 2004 over a) the possibility of Las Vegas–style casinos coming to the UK and b) a government ban on hunting. This, however, wasn't a case of manufacturing hysteria, as it was with the dangerous dogs business – there were clearly lots of people out there genuinely opposed to both.

The media can also be a huge factor in ministerial resignations. This was recently the case with both Stephen Byers, the Minister for Transport, and Peter Mandelson, who was 'got' twice: once while he was Minister for Trade, and then again as Northern Ireland Secretary.

So in conclusion: yes, the media have a lot of power. The power to influence. And that's a very big power indeed.

14. EUROPE

Whether you like it or not, Europe has quite a few tanks on our lawn. When the Conservative PM Edward Heath signed the European Communities Act 1972, our control over certain things started to evaporate, like boiling water off rice. It's been carrying on ever since. The EU regularly issues things called 'directives' and 'regulations', which can then become part of our law. Now that's what I call power.

But is Europe's power over us a good thing? Blimey. Now you're asking. I need a whole chapter for that one. And it's coming up next.

15. AMERICA

It's very hard not to escape the conclusion that we only went to war with Iraq in 2003 because the Americans wanted us to. Which, in my eyes, makes them very powerful indeed, despite Tony Blair's claim that: 'Britain's place is at the heart of Europe.'

Maybe he meant Europe, Alabama.

We have, of course, famously had a 'Special Relationship' with the Yanks for years. The flirting started in earnest during WWII, when the American President Franklin D. Roosevelt joined with Winston Churchill and helped save the free world. The petting got really heavy in the mid-1980s – Ronald Reagan and Margaret Thatcher hit it off from the beginning. The relationship between their successors, George Bush Sr. and John Major, was a lot cooler. Things warmed up considerably again, though, with Bill Clinton and Tony Blair. Staff from Bill's campaign team even helped Tony win the election in 1997.

So it didn't look good when George W. Bush got in. He disliked a lot of what Tony's mate, Bill Clinton, stood for. It looked even worse when George W. greeted the Mexican President thus: 'The United States has no more important relationship in the world than the one we have with... Mexico.'

But then came 9/11 and Tony Blair's declaration that we stood 'shoulder to shoulder' with the USA. (Let's not be cynical and wonder whether George W. would have reacted the same way if 9/11 had happened to us.) The Special Relationship was immediately back in business. Our PM was described in the US media as 'America's chief foreign ambassador' and 'America's closest ally'.

And there was something else that brought the two leaders even closer together: religion. Both are fully fledged members of the God Squad.

But is there really a Special Relationship? It's been said the reason the relationship is special is because only one side knows it exists. And it's certainly quite unequal: we have surrendered a lot of sovereignty to the US, and not got much in return. In 1948, for example, the Labour government invited American nuclear bombers to set up bases in Britain. They've been here ever since, which means if there was ever a WWIII, we'd be an automatic participant.

At the moment then, the US holds a mighty sway over Us. But some say it shouldn't. They point out that the US has several other close relationships on the go, including those with Japan and Canada. And, in particular, Israel. Oh, and Mexico of course. And that they're only nice to us when it suits them. And that it would be much healthier if we really *did* take our place at the heart of Europe, so there would be an alternative centre of power in the world.

Things might change, though. The next PM after Tony Blair might not be so lovey-dovey with the USA. And Britain has agreed to begin joint military planning with the European Union. That hardly represents the end of the Special Relationship: it's more like agreeing to – maybe – go for a coffee with someone else, sometime in the future. It might just be the start of the beginning of the end. But I doubt it.

16. THE PRIME MINISTER

... is the most powerful person in the land (though see 17, below). I know, I know: I am becoming a Professor of the Bleeding Obvious. But it's worth sketching out just how powerful. If he or she has :

1. a dominant personality and
2. a very large majority in the House of Commons;

they are up there with God in the power stakes. Mrs Thatcher had both 1. and 2. She was strong, bossy and knew what she wanted. Tony Blair has certainly enjoyed 2., so he can do pretty much what he wants. The only problem is that no one really knows exactly *what* he wants, apart from power, grinning a lot and taking us to war. However, John Major, Tory PM for five years, had neither 1. nor 2., and so his power amounted to little more than setting up a Motorway Cones Hotline.

Tony Blair gave a nice little insight into the job in his speech at the 1998 Labour Party conference: 'When you become Prime Minister, the first thing they do after telling you how to launch the nuclear bomb is take your passport from you, and then the rest of the time trying to get you to travel around the world.' After he'd found out how to press the button, by the way, he was introduced to the staff and shown round. He found a bottle of champagne from his predecessor, John Major. The note with it, addressed to Tony and Cherie, read: 'It's a great job – enjoy it.'

In football terms, the PM picks the team and decides the tactics. There is no fat, sweaty chairman waiting in the wings with his finger hovering over the ejector button. The only people who can get rid of him are the fans – ie us – or himself. Harold Wilson, for example, mysteriously resigned as PM in 1976. (To this day nobody is quite sure why, but one theory is that he realized he was suffering from the early stages of senile dementia). Oh, and the PM can also be got rid of by a vote of no confidence from the House of Commons.

The PM appoints all the government's senior ministers. He decides who is going to be in his Cabinet and controls the agenda for its meetings. He also appoints junior ministers, senior civil servants, bishops, judges and heads of inquiries. (This last one is quite important, which is why I am devoting a whole chapter to it later on.) The PM can also sack any of the above.

The PM can make entire government departments vanish if he wants to – by joining two of them together, or simply by disbanding one. He can also invent new ones. He represents the UK abroad at important meetings and summits. And he can call a general election when he damn well likes – as long as it's within five years of him entering into office. He can also – incredibly – lead us into a war, even if we don't want one…

Indeed, it was the 'Iraq business' that made many people worry that the PM was simply too powerful and that it wasn't very fair or democratic for so much decision-making ability to be vested in one person. But then again, we hold the ultimate trump card over King Tony: we can chuck him out. And he's not the first person to be accused of being too powerful. Come in Harold Wilson and Margaret Thatcher.

It's the way we make 'em, I'm afraid: over the years, because of the way our (unwritten) constitution has developed, more and more power has flowed into the prime ministerial cup. Verily, it now runneth over. What's to be done? Well, if we had a written constitution, it might help. We could then set down on paper definite limits on the PM's power. Failing that, we could always start a revolution. But I can't see the people of Tunbridge Wells going for that.

17. THE CHANCELLOR

... is more powerful than the Prime Minister: discuss.

Well, you could say that – and easily keep a straight face. After all, the Chancellor runs the economy, and the economy is everything. Hence the famous American election-winning phrase: 'It's the economy, stupid.'

It's the Chancellor who decides how much money is going to be spent, and where. He is, arguably, the overlord of all things domestic: from pensions to policemen, from transport to trade policy. He can exert control over every government department and every single minister.

Like I said before, much depends on the personalities involved. And right now, because of the type of bloke Gordon Brown is, the Chancellor of the Exchequer has never been more powerful. Too powerful, according to the *Guardian* in April 2002: 'Too large a chunk of Whitehall has been colonised by the Chancellor.'

So why is this chancellor, in particular, so mighty? Well, for a kick-off, he's got two brains. Once, for example, he started going on about something called 'neo-classical endogenous growth theory'. No one knew what that meant, of course. But that was the point: it was terribly impressive. He also went about making the Treasury – and therefore himself – more powerful as soon as he got in. One way he did this was by changing the recruitment policy. Instead of letting the civil service machine employ staff for him, he got the Treasury to do it separately. They only gave jobs to the brightest and the best. And what's the best recipe for success and power? It's the people, stupid.

Interestingly, only three chancellors since the war – Harold Macmillan, James Callaghan and John Major – have gone on to be Prime Minister. None of the really successful ones, ie the ones that made a mark – Roy Jenkins, Denis Healey, Nigel Lawson – went on to get the top job.

Right. It's time to talk about Europe. Don't go away.

CHAPTER SEVEN

A Flood of Paedophiles

This chapter should really be called: 'Europe – What's it all About?', but I was worried a title like that would put you off. Like a three-hour lecture on particle physics or an edition of *Panorama*, I always thought the issue of Europe was 1) boring, 2) confusing and 3) of no relevance to my everyday life.

And I'm not the only one. There have been loads of opinion polls showing that millions of ordinary people know very little about Europe and care even less. That's why nearly 80 per cent of us couldn't be arsed to vote in the European elections of 1999, thereby creating a record for the lowest turnout ever. Compare this with the Maltese, the most enthusiastic Europeans on the planet. More than eight out of ten of them raced down to the polling booths for the Euro elections of 2004.

Someone hasn't told the British press this, however. For many papers, Europe = a headline a day. But then, many of those papers have owners with a vested interest in slagging Europe off. Take the *Sun*, which sells 3 million copies – and is read by up to 10 million people – every day. The *Sun* feels the same way about pro-Europeans as the rest of us do about people who club seals to death. Take the following *Sun* headline, from 5 November 2003: 'EU PERVS ALERT'. The gist of the story was that Britain was in danger of being flooded with paedophiles, because of the European Union. The story pointed out that ten countries were about to join, and so their citizens would be able to move around Europe much more freely. But many of those ten new countries didn't keep sex offenders registers. So euro pervs would be free to come to Britain and molest our kids. This story wasn't 100 per cent wrong; it cunningly used words such as 'could' rather than 'will' when it talked about the likelihood of the perv invasion. But it was alarmist, selective and a bit irrational. (Mind you: show me a journalist who claims not to have been any of those things, ever, and I'll show you a liar.)

The *Sun* has also charged the EU with, among other things, wanting to ban rocking horses, tax Remembrance Day poppies and rename Waterloo Station to avoid offending the French. These stories are all quite entertaining, but like the 'flood of paedophiles' tale, misleading. The *Sun* has an agenda, however. It's owned by Rupert Murdoch and Rupert doesn't like Europe very much, as the closer the UK gets to it, the harder it will be for him to expand his media empire and make more money. The *Sun* would argue that when it slags off Europe, it's only reflecting what its readers think, which may well be true. But it's also a very convenient excuse.

Anyway, the *Sun* isn't the only one obsessed with Europe. Politicians are too. Especially the Tories. They lost the general election of 2001, and are about to lose the next one, because they believe – mistakenly – that lots of us care deeply about things like European fishing quotas. They are so convinced that Europe is A Big Issue for voters that in early 2004 they tried to get opinion polls carried out to prove it. But at least two polling firms turned them down, as they resented feeling pressured to come up with the 'right' conclusion, ie that we all care deeply about Europe. Oh dear.

For the rest of us, though, Europe is boring. Let's face it, how many people do you know who stay awake at night fretting about the European Constitution? That doesn't mean it's not important, though. It is. And I was wrong to say it doesn't affect our everyday lives. It does. You just haven't realised it, that's all. In fact if you like the seaside, Pret A Manger and travelling, Europe affects you hugely, because:

1. IT'S MADE OUR BEACHES CLEANER

There are, thank God, very few turds floating in our sea these days. And for that we must thank Europe. A decade ago, half our beaches failed to meet European standards. Today, more than 98 per cent of them do, and they proudly possess something called the Blue Flag as a result. It's not just our beaches. The European Union did away with leaded petrol in 2000, which meant an end to unpleasant and harmful emissions (from cars, not newspapers). If you're a tree hugger, the EU is good news.

2. IT'S MADE TRIPS TO PRET A MANGER/McDONALD'S/THE PUB VERY FRUSTRATING INDEED

We've all been there: you ask the bloke behind the counter at Pret A Manger whether there are any crunchy caramel cheesecakes left, and he gives you a blank look.

You ask again. Ditto. It turns out he is Polish or Latvian or Greek and doesn't understand a word you're saying. This is because we now have a thing called European citizenship – as indicated by your nice burgundy-coloured passport – which means anyone from over there can work over here. And vice versa. If you live in a country that is in the European Union you have the right to work in any of the other 24 member states without a visa. That means you could be flipping burgers right now in Austria, Belgium, Cyprus, the Czech Republic, Denmark, Estonia, Finland, France, Germany, Greece, Hungary, Ireland, Italy, Latvia, Lithuania, Luxembourg, Malta, the Netherlands, Poland, Portugal, Slovakia, Slovenia, Spain or Sweden. (If you fancy working in Romania, Bulgaria, Turkey or Croatia, by the way, don't worry – they should be coming on stream soon.)

3. IT'S MADE TRAVELLING AROUND EUROPE MUCH LESS OF A KERFUFFLE

Because 12 countries now have the same currency – the euro – you don't have to change money every time you cross a border. That means you can now visit Austria, Belgium, Finland, France, Germany, Greece, Ireland, Italy, Luxembourg, the Netherlands, Portugal and Spain without having to use rip-off money-changers once. A euro, by the way, is worth around 70p. At least, it was when this book was written.

You might not know it, but the EU has also had a big effect on the way we work. Thanks to some scintillatingly interesting Euro legislation, many of us now do shorter hours, have longer holidays and are safer at work.

Mind you, when this whole thing started, turds in the sea, workers' rights and burgundy passports weren't on anyone's agenda. That was in 1952, when six countries got together to form – pay attention now, it could come up in a pub quiz – the European Coal and Steel Community. The thinking back then was that if we form a cosy little club, and give each other special deals on things such as coal and steel, it should make us closer and prevent another world war.

The UK, however, didn't join the party until 1973, after we'd signed the Treaty of Brussels. That happened under Edward Heath, a Conservative prime minister who liked yachts, guffawing and being a bachelor. Before that we'd spent the 1960s trying, and failing, to gatecrash the party. Our lack of success was mainly due to the French leader, Charles de Gaulle. He's the man with the shortest catchphrase in history – 'Non' – which is what he said every time we asked to join.

Right, that's the history out of the way. Now, let's say you are at a dinner party, in the pub, or with the in-laws, and someone brings up the subject of Europe. You have three choices. You can tilt your head slightly to one side and give it your best 'Mmm, that's really interesting' look. You can develop a fascination for the label on the wine bottle in front of you. Or you can attempt to make a valid contribution – in which case, this next bit is for you.

WHY EURO LOVERS LOVE EUROPE AND WHY EURO HATERS HATE IT

1. IT KEEPS LOADS OF US IN WORK AND MAKES SOME OF US VERY RICH INDEED

EURO LOVERS SAY: We do an awful lot of business with Europe. In one year, British companies can easily sell £100 billion worth of stuff to Europe. One hundred billion pounds is a lot of money, a lot of trade and a lot of jobs. If we weren't signed up to Europe, we would lose billions of pounds' worth of those deals. The reason why we sell so much to European customers is because they get favourable deals on the stuff we make, and vice versa. We have unlimited access to the largest and richest market in the world: and because we are fully fledged members of it, we get special tax privileges. If we left the EU tomorrow, around a million jobs would be at risk.

EURO HATERS SAY: You've got a point there. But even if we left the EU we'd still do business with Europe, just not quite as much. And we could then find other countries to do more deals with, such as America.

2. WE GET LOTS OF FREE MONEY FROM EUROPE

EURO LOVERS SAY: Have you ever been to Liverpool? The docks used to be a shithole. But then they did it up, using tens of millions of pounds in European grants. As a result, Liverpool Docks is now very tasty − bars, cafés, yuppie flats, the lot − and

131

thousands of people now have jobs who previously didn't. The same goes for towns and cities all over Britain: Newcastle, Cornwall, Birmingham and even parts of the South-East have had millions of euros spent on them.

EURO HATERS SAY: Yeah, but pumping loads of money into shitholes only works in the short term. No matter how much you spend, the poorer bits of the UK will always stay that way, compared to the richer bits. And anyway, we might get a lot of money off the EU, but we always end up giving them a whole lot more. In 2004, for example, we are going to end up giving the EU £4 *billion* more than we get from it. £4 billion, incidentally, is what Greece makes from it, in a good year. We could have spent that on ourselves, instead of effectively donating it to the Greeks. Not exactly fair, is it?

3. IT'S MADE OUR QUALITY OF LIFE A WHOLE LOT BETTER

EURO LOVERS SAY: Thanks to Europe a lot of us do shorter hours, get decent holidays, and are much safer at work. Our air is purer and our beaches are cleaner. Put that in your unleaded exhaust pipe and smoke it. And anyway, in this world you're no one unless you're in a gang. That's why there are so many of them. Take FTAA (the Free Trade Area of the Americas: 34 countries). And look at APEC (Asia Pacific Cooperation: 21 members). Not forgetting MERCOSUR, of course (Mercado

Comun del Sur, or the Southern Common Market: nine members). Strength – and safety – comes in numbers.

EURO HATERS SAY: Being in a gang makes good sense. But not this gang. There are others we could join. What's more, we'd have done that clean air stuff anyway, whether we'd been in the EU or not.

4. WE HAVE LOST THE ABILITY TO CONTROL OUR OWN AFFAIRS.

EURO HATERS SAY: This is the big one. It's about the 'S' word. We are losing our sovereignty. We are letting people who don't have our best interests at heart control our destiny. If the EU passes a law we have no choice but to go along with it. We can say no to them occasionally, when they pass laws about things like taxation and defence, as we have a veto in those areas. But the way things are going we might even lose that.

EURO LOVERS SAY: Sovereignty is a bit like virginity. Once you've lost it you can't get it back. And we lost ours in 1973, when we joined up. That was part of the deal, so get over it, pal. We may have given up some power to Brussels, but it hasn't exactly done us any harm, has it? There are far more pluses – jobs, trade deals, clean beaches etc. – than minuses.

5. ALL THAT RED TAPE – IT'S A BUREAUCRATIC NIGHTMARE

EURO HATERS SAY: British businesses are being strangled by European red tape. Daft Euro rules cost us time, money and even jobs. It's ridiculous. Take Peter Robinson, a Welsh newsagent, who axed all his newspaper rounds after 35 years. The main reason was something called the European Union Young Workers Directive 94/33, which made it virtually impossible for him to employ school kids. It required him to: 1) register them with the local authority; 2) get written permission from their schools; 3) fill out a dreaded 'health-and-safety risk-assessment form' for each one; and 4) give holiday and sick pay to anyone under 16. Not surprisingly, he thought, 'Forget it,' and stopped deliveries altogether. Red tape like this costs British businesses several hundred million pounds every year.

EURO LOVERS SAY: Get real. Any form of government needs rules or there'd be a free-for-all. And the EU needs more rules than most, as it has 25 countries, each with its own rules, some of which contradict each other. So new rules will always be needed to make sure things work smoothly. Anyway – rules are there to protect people and avoid unfairness.

6) THE WHOLE THING IS FRAUDULENT AND CORRUPT

EURO HATERS SAY: It's a gravy train, and a bent one at that. In 2003, it's reckoned 500 million quid was swindled out of the EU. Favourite scams include expense fiddles, claiming money for work that hasn't been done and siphoning vast sums of money into personal bank accounts. Occasionally they are at least imaginative: somebody in Croatia once claimed a huge grant for the country's sugar cane industry. It was later found out that sugar cane doesn't even grow in Croatia. Things got so bad that in 1999, all of the big cheeses representing all the EU countries – the so-called commissioners – resigned en masse, after allegations of mismanagement and nepotism.

EURO LOVERS SAY: At least they had the decency to resign. When did a group of British politicians last resign after cocking up? Yes, there is too much fraud. But get it in perspective. Five hundred million quid seems a lot, but it's only 1 per cent of the EU budget. The UK recently lost ten times that amount – nearly 5 billion quid in social security fraud, in one year. And at least the EU are committed to stamping it out.

7. THE C.A.P. IS C.R.A.P.

EURO HATERS SAY: The Common Agricultural Policy? Don't get us started. It's obscene. Farmers all over Europe get paid tens of millions of pounds, in so-called subsidies, to help them keep their prices down, and to protect them from competition. Sometimes they get paid huge amounts of money just to do nothing. Things are now so bad that European farmers receive an average subsidy of £1.30 a day for every cow they own. That's twice the daily average wage of more than one billion human beings. So thanks to the CAP, cows now earn more than some humans. No wonder the Chancellor, Gordon Brown, reckons the system is evil.

EURO LOVERS SAY: Er… not good, is it? We'll give you that one. We are least trying to reform the CAP. But these things take time.

★ ★ ★ ★ ★

If things get too heated at the dinner party, you could always get straight to the point. Try saying something like: 'The only issue here is whether we give Europe the power to set our taxes for us. Pass the chocolates, please.'

The issue of 'tax harmonisation', as it's called, is the Really Big European Issue. If we give the EU the power to set our taxes, then we will lose the thing we value most: the ability to control our own finances. Tax harmonisation would also mean us paying more tax. Eek. One of the Chancellor's brainiest boffins, Professor Tim Congdon, did a big study on this. He reckoned harmonisation would mean us paying up to 30 per cent more tax, over a period of ten years.

So what are the odds on Europe-wide tax harmonisation happening? Not surprisingly, it depends who you talk to. The Euro haters say it's a very real threat, given that the French and the Germans openly admit that they want it. Euro lovers say, 'Don't worry, it isn't going to happen. For a start, the Chancellor, Gordon Brown, says there is no need for it and it is certainly not a priority.' They also point out that the UK has an ultimate veto on tax matters.

But the Euro haters say that veto could easily be lost: it's happened before. Back in 1987, Lady Thatcher, who was then our PM, agreed to the Single European Act. In doing so, she gave away our right of veto on a number of issues. Apparently, it only dawned on the poor old dear a few years later that she'd given away a huge amount of our power.

But a lot of things would have to happen before we lost ultimate control over our own finances. For a start, we would have to join the euro, ie the Single European Currency. And we wouldn't do that without a referendum. At the moment, there's no sign of that happening. But it might well do in the next few years. If it does, the politicians will probably go round saying: 'Don't worry, there's no way a vote for the euro will mean higher taxes.'

But you might not want to believe them. The last time they said something like that was in 1972, when we were about to join the Common Market. Back then, people worried that we were going to lose our sovereignty. The politicians' response was: 'Don't be silly, of course we won't.' They were wrong. We did lose our sovereignty. Who says they won't mislead us again, next time round, when it comes to the tax issue?

There is a way round this, of course: the Ultimate Euro Haters' way. We could pull out of Europe. Then there's no way the EU could set our taxes. That's what the United Kingdom Independence Party (UKIP) wants, and quite a few people agree with them. At the Euro Elections in 2004, they got more than two and half million votes. But pulling out of Europe is a bit like reversing a vasectomy: it's possible in theory. But it's expensive, painful and it might not work.

So what happens next? Well, there's a 'yes' or 'no' referendum coming in the next few years, on the European Constitution. At least, that's what Tony Blair has promised. So there might be. This is unlikely to have people flocking to the voting booths in their millions though, as it's not a very sexy issue and hardly anyone understands what it's about anyway. If you don't believe me, take a look at the full text of the European constitution. It's on the internet. A word of warning though: you may lose the will to live. It's 265 pages long and a bit of an Euro jargon fest. If you're determined, however, my advice is to take it a paragraph at a time. Treat each one like those weird, fuzzy pictures they used to print in newspaper supplements. You know, the ones that looked like an incoherent mass of dots and coloured smudges. At first you couldn't make any sense of them at

all. But if you stared long enough and hard enough, an image of sorts would evenutally begin to emerge. So it is with the draft text of the European Constitution. Anyway, whatever the result of the referendum, it won't really make a big difference to our lives. It will, though, serve as a useful opinion poll on the subject, so politicians can see which way the wind is blowing.

In the meantime, we will carry on doing the hokey cokey on Europe. We will put our left leg in, our right leg out, and then when it comes to things like referendums, we'll do the hokey cokey and shake it all about. This, I think, is what they mean by a twin-speed Europe. We are clearly in a slightly slower lane than the French and the Germans, who love Europe to bits. We're not quite so sure. But we like it that way, don't we?

Now let's get back closer to home. I've another question. Which is …

CHAPTER EIGHT

Why Are
There Only
Two Parties
to Choose
From?

Yes, yes, I know: there are dozens of parties. There's the Liberal Democrats, the Greens, the BNP, UKIP, the Monster Raving Loony-type outfits and loads more. But since the war, only two parties – Labour and Conservative – have actually held power. That may change, one day, but in the meantime it's worth investigating a) whether it's a good thing and b) how it's come about.

First things first. There are – apparently – only two main parties to choose from because of our voting system. It lends itself, massively, to there being just the Big Two. British elections use something called the 'first past the post' system and it is, arguably, hugely undemocratic and unfair. That's because it can produce weird results, where the winning party actually gets *fewer* votes than the losing one. Yes, you read that right. We have a system where, potentially, the loser wins. Imagine if that the case were used in football. The side coming second in the Premier League would pick up the title, while the team that actually finished with the most points would go home empty handed.

That's pretty much what happened in February 1974: the Conservatives got 150,000 more votes than Labour, but lost because Labour had more seats. The party that wins the election has the most seats in the House of Commons, not necessarily the most votes. That means that everything depends on geographical patterns, and the way the parties' votes are distributed across the country.

Lets say it's election time in the constituency of

Chipping Sodbury and 51,000 people vote. There are five candidates to choose from. The Tory gets 11,000 votes, and the other four candidates get roughly 10,000 each. The Tory wins the seat, of course, because he's got the most votes. So far, so fair. But think about it. Every single one of the votes cast for the four other candidates – all 40,000 of them – has, effectively, been wasted. Eighty per cent of the voters have been ignored. Their democratic voice has gone unheard.

Now, say that pattern is repeated in towns and cities across the country – ie the Tories have just enough votes to scrape by in 350 seats. Because there are only 660-odd seats up for grabs, they would have a healthy majority in the House of Commons: 350 seats, as opposed to the rest having only 300 between them. So the Tories get in for five years, and do what they like, even though *four-fifths* of the electorate have voted against them, and hate everything they stand for.

That, for better or worse, is the system we have. It's biased in favour of one or other of the two major parties, but none of the others. It's a bit of a stitch-up, really. It limits your choice. It can also put you in the strange position of voting for a party whose policies you dislike. Say you marginally fancy the Tories over Labour. But you don't like the look of some Tory policies at all. You think their stand on health and education is laughable. So you wrestle with your conscience, but realise you've got to vote Tory, reluctantly, because you hate Labour policies even more. So you end up voting for a party with policies you can't stand. No wonder Winston Churchill said: 'No one pretends that democracy is perfect ... indeed it has been said that democracy is the worst form of government, except all those other forms that have been tried from time to time.'

Even the design of the House of Commons itself is biased in favour of the big two: it's narrow and rectangular, and therefore ideally suited for one party to sit on one side, and the other to sit opposite. Architecturally – and politically – there ain't room for a third. That's why some of the newer political debating chambers – for example, the one at the European Parliament – are circular. The politicians are discouraged from immediately taking sides – because there aren't any. As a result, it's said, the policies – like the chamber – are more rounded. At Westminster, on the other hand, MPs are often forced to take the opposite view, even if there isn't one, because the system rewards them for doing so.

But people who swear by the 'first past the post' system say there are several good things about it. For a kick-off, there's the Abba Argument. Because 'The Winner Takes It All', the winning party doesn't have to keep taking account of what the runner-up thinks, which makes for strong, decisive governments. The system also delivers a quick result, and is simple for the voters to understand. And it provides a clear, visible democratic link between the people and Parliament: every voter is represented by a living, breathing local MP (not that you'd know by looking at some of them).

And there's more. Because the system tends to be less topsy-turvy and volatile in terms of election results, governments stay in power for longer. The Tories, for example, were in for 18 years up to 1997, and Labour have so far clocked up seven. (And if you believe the bookies, another five is a formality.) That, it's argued, makes for experienced, better, governments, as they get sufficient time to get to grips with the job. Others might think the opposite, mind you: the longer a government is in power, the more complacent, arrogant and out of touch it gets.

And another thing. The alternative to the 'first past the post' system would be some kind of Proportional Representation (PR). There are several types of PR, including the Additional Member System, the Alternative Vote System, and the Single Transferable Vote System (STV). I won't go into the details of each one, as it might make your head explode. The STV system, in particular, is about as easy to understand as an Albanian Airways in-flight training manual. But the long and the short of these systems is that basically, if a party got 42 per cent of the votes (like Labour did in 2001) then it would get around 42 per cent of the seats, give or take a few. But that could easily mean a never-ending stream of inconclusive election results, where no single party had a clear overall majority. That would mean deals might have to be done with minority parties. And in theory, that could mean some decidedly dodgy smaller parties holding huge amounts of power. Take, for instance, the following election result:

Labour:	42 per cent
Tory:	42 per cent
Liberal Democrat:	7.5 per cent
British National Party:	8.5 per cent

Under a system of PR, a party would need 50 per cent of the votes to form a government. So in this situation, one option for Labour or the Tories would be to form a partnership with the BNP, as their 8.5 per cent of the vote would take either party beyond the magic 50 per cent mark.

Then again, PR fans would argue, the above situation would never arise. The BNP will never get 8 per cent of the vote, not in a month of Sundays. And even if they did, the British people simply wouldn't tolerate a mainstream party doing a deal like that. But fans of the system argue that PR is a massive force for good, as it makes everyone take account of everyone else's views. If things are going to happen, compromises have to be made. Which means more people's views are going to be taken into account. Which is what democracy is all about, surely.

So what are the chances of PR happening, then? Not much. If the big two parties voted to change our electoral system, they would, in effect, be delivering a hammer blow to their chances of running the country single-handedly. These turkeys ain't gonna vote for Christmas. Having said that, Tony Blair has flirted with the idea, and even got his mate, the late Lord (Roy) Jenkins to come up with a report on the whole issue, which was very well received. But then Labour did disastrously in the Euro Elections of 2004, which used a system of... PR. And now, for some reason, voting reform doesn't seem to be anywhere near the top of the prime ministerial in-tray.

But we can't blame everything on our voting system. That's not the only reason there have always been two dominant parties. Another factor — a more important one, really — is that it's simply a reflection of what's been happening out there. For a long time, society — and politics — was basically split into two broad camps. There were no stools to fall between: you had to choose between one or the other. You were either rich, or at least reasonably well off (Tory), or poor (Labour). You were either working class (Labour) or middle/upper class (Tory). You wanted the government to run the electricity, gas, phone and train services (Labour) or you didn't (Tory). You wanted to get rid of our nuclear weapons (Labour, in 1983) or you didn't. There wasn't room for anyone else. This domination of the Big Two — similar to the Arsenal/Manchester United scenario over recent years — reached its height in 1970, when more than 90 per cent of the seats contested in the election were straight two-way contests between Labour and Conservative.

But then things started to change. By the 1990s, it wasn't a case of being either working class or upper class. Suddenly, an awful lot of us seemed to be stuck in the middle. Hence Tony Blair's famous observation that 'We're all middle class now.' And most of us decided that we would, for better or worse, actually prefer things like the trains, gas, electricity and phones to be run privately, thank you very much. No differences between the Big Two parties on that issue, then. Gradually, the distinctions that made the Tories Tory and Labour Labour started to evaporate. The big new issues – the environment, health, education – had nothing to do with old party rivalries. Both the Big Two liked them and wanted to spend lots of money on them. So it was no longer a simple case of being in one camp or the other.

In other words, the dominance of the Big Two may, at last, be on the slide. For a start, a Medium-Sized Three has been coming up on the rails – namely the Liberal Democrats and the Welsh and Scottish Nationalists. The Lib Dems got 52 seats at the election of 2001 – their best result for ages. And the Nationalists have come from Nowhere to Somewhere in the space of twenty-odd years. That's why, in 1992, the percentage of seats that were direct two-way contests between Labour and the Conservatives was 65 per cent. Twenty years earlier, remember, it had been 90 per cent. Which suggests that, although the two-party system isn't crumbling, it may have started fraying at the edges.

So here's the question. Could it happen? Could the

stranglehold of the Big Two be permanently broken? Well, it seems to have happened in football. For Labour, Tory and the Lib Dems, read Arsenal, Manchester United and Chelsea respectively. Not the most impressive piece of evidence, I admit, but you know what I mean. Maybe there's a better comparison: broadcasting. Once, the TV jungle, like its political equivalent, was dominated by two all-powerful 800lb gorillas. Just like Labour and the Conservatives, ITV and the BBC had the whole place to themselves. They could do whatever they liked. But just like Labour and the Conservatives, the BBC and ITV didn't realise the jungle was changing and that people wanted something different. Instead of reacting to the imminent threat of hundreds of smaller, nimbler, special-interest TV channels, they carried on eating bananas and got fat, bloated and complacent. As a result, audiences for ITV and the BBC have been decimated. Could it be that the Big Two political parties have been similarly short-sighted, and not spotted the dangers posed by hundreds of smaller, nimbler, special-interest groups?

We've been here before. Over the years, plenty of people have predicted the demise of the Big Two's stranglehold. Cue – many times over – the phrase 'The tectonic plates of British politics are shifting.' But, to dismiss that cliché with another, reports of the death of the two-party system have, so far, proved greatly exaggerated. Many people thought the earthquake was starting in 1981, when a brand new party, the SDP, promised to break the mould of British politics. It never happened. Some pundits are again saying that the plates might well be shifting now, following the Tories' historically bad rogering in the elections of 1997 and 2001. In the past, these pundits point out, whenever the Tories have taken a heavy beating (eg the elections of 1906, 1945 and 1966) they bounced back strongly, straight away, in the very next election. But look! This time it's different. They got stuffed good and proper in 1997… only to get stuffed good and proper again, in 2001. So maybe, these experts are saying, it *is* finally happening. Maybe it's no longer a case of the Big Two. Maybe we're down to a Big One and a Half. Or maybe the Lib Dems are about to do even better this time around. In which case we'll be up to a Big Two and a Half. Or even a Big Three. Interesting times!

Let's not forget, however, that Labour have been in intensive care too, just like the Tories are now, and managed to come back. In 1983 they were obliterated. It was the first of *three* election whuppings on the trot. But they still bounced back gloriously in 1997. The Tories may be in deep doggy doo-doos, but they're no worse off now, than Labour were in 1983. And unlike Labour, the Tories haven't managed to lose three elections on the trot… yet.

It is going to be dead tricky for the Tories to make a decent comeback, though. And they know it. Part of the problem is that every time they come up with a different policy or promising idea, New Labour nicks it. Take the

Tory brainwave of trimming back fat government, ie sacking loads of civil servants. People liked it. So what did Labour do? They stole it. In the budget of 2004, Gordon Brown announced he was getting rid of tens of thousands of government jobs. Then there was one of the Tory big ideas of the early 1990s: Public Private Partnerships (PPPs). This involved building things for the public good – such as schools, hospitals and transport projects – using a lot of private expertise and money.

Labour nicked that one too. As a result, the Tories are finding it mighty hard to offer the British public something new. And they've also got a huge problem with UKIP, the anti-Europe party, who are nicking votes off them left, right and centre. But mainly right.

You never know. The tectonic plates of British politics might not be shifting ... but there are definitely a few tremors.

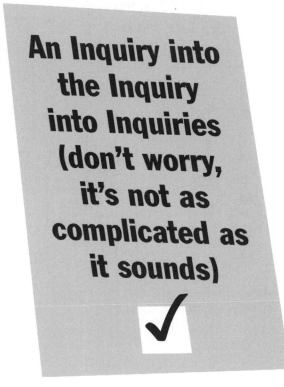

CHAPTER NINE

An Inquiry into
the Inquiry
into Inquiries
(don't worry,
it's not as
complicated as
it sounds)

You are the Prime Minister. There's been a cock-up/scandal/war/controversy. The slavering dogs of the press are wild-eyed and hungry for blood. Preferably yours, or that of someone in your government. The opposition party is making a three-course meal out of it. And the public thinks something needs to be done. What do you do? You throw them a bone. You announce that there is going to be − roll on the drums, please! − a full public inquiry.

If you're a PM in trouble, inquiries can be wonderful things. They are brilliant at lancing the boil. Once you've announced it, the press will have something to write about and the TV news will have their lead story. Then the whole media circus will pack up its tent and move on. Your troublesome issue has been dealt with − until, that is, the result of the inquiry is made public. But by that time most ordinary people will have forgotten what the whole thing was about in the first place. And even if they haven't, the inquiry will almost certainly find you, and anyone else in your government connected with the affair, either innocent or just-a-little-bit-guilty-but-don't-worry-it's-not-a-resigning-matter.

This may have something to do with the fact that you, the PM, are in the enviable position of being able to set the terms of reference for the inquiry. That means it's down to you to decide the rules of the game. Even better, you also have the power to decide who should hold it. That's like someone who's been accused of burglary being allowed to choose the judge and members of the jury. If the person in charge of the inquiry has the PM to thank for putting them there, what are the chances of them being 100 per cent fair? I'm not saying that judges who hold big inquiries say to themselves, 'Hmm. The PM gave me this excellent job and there is bound to be a knighthood in it so there's no way I am going to be hard on him.' But then again, judges are like the rest of us: they have a subconscious. And they're not overly given to biting the hand that feeds.

In the last 20 years, we've gone inquiry crazy. Instead of saving them up for special occasions, we're having one into just about everything. Such as the police investigation into the murder of a black teenager (the Macpherson Inquiry). Such as the Tory government's selling of arms to Iraq (the Scott Inquiry). Such as the army's killing of 14 unarmed Catholics during the troubles in Ulster (the Bloody Sunday Inquiry). At this rate it won't be too long before they hold an inquiry into why we're holding so many inquiries. Hold on a minute. They already have. I'm not joking. It started in 2004.

One thing the inquiry into inquiries might like to ask is this: how can we stop some of these inquiries turning into epic wastes of time and money? One, in particular, has become a complete fiasco: the Bloody Sunday Inquiry. It's been going on so long that some of the people involved in it have died. It's so far taken six years, called 900 witnesses and cost £150 million. It's reckoned it could cost as much as £250 million. And what will it have achieved when it's all over? It will have made an awful lot of lawyers and barristers richer than they could ever have imagined.

But the most famous – notorious, for some – inquiry of recent times was Hutton's, in 2004, which looked into the suicide of weapons expert Dr David Kelly before the Iraq War. Most experts agreed that both parties under investigation – the BBC and the government – had made serious mistakes. The BBC had falsely accused the government of lying. But there was also plenty of evidence to show that the government was indeed guilty of the more general charge of sexing up the intelligence about Iraq's nuclear weapons. And its behaviour in the chain of events that led to the naming of Dr Kelly as the source of the key BBC story was, many felt, morally questionable. The verdict, everyone agreed, would be 'a plague on both your houses.' In footballing terms, it would be a messy score draw.

The proceedings were chaired by a bloke who had been made a lord by – surprise, surprise – Tony Blair. Throughout the inquiry's proceedings, Lord Hutton's relationship with the PM resembled that of a public school fag with his prefect. When Lord H explained why he'd decided not to call the PM back to give evidence for a second time, he said he did not think it was 'appropriate' to do so. For someone who's supposed to be holding a fair and ruthlessly balanced inquiry, that shows an almost unhealthy level of respect for the PM. Lord H should have been playing the role of headmaster, not fag: in which case he would have called the PM back, and given him another bloody good grilling. Or at the very least, a light simmering. Tony Blair, after all, was the man with ultimate control over the whole sorry affair. But Lord H seemed to think it was his duty not to.

The verdict shocked everyone. It wasn't the draw everyone was expecting, but 5-0 to the government. The PM came out looking like the Angel Gabriel. But we shouldn't have been surprised. As far as most public inquiries are concerned, 'twas ever thus.

British public inquiries have a habit of weighing up the evidence carefully, on both sides, and then either finding in favour of the government, or doing nothing. The trend started more than forty years ago, when Lord Denning looked into the Profumo Affair. Lord D failed to do the one thing judges are supposed to do: judge. The only thing resembling a firm conclusion in this report was his observation that the government could have dealt with the whole thing – a sex scandal – more quickly. Disappointingly, he also failed to identify the famous 'Man in the Mask', a naked gent who kept popping up during Mr Profumo's extracurricular activities. (The rumours were that it was a cabinet minister.) Mind you, Denning's timidity didn't harm sales: remarkably, 100,000 copies of the report were bought within three days of it being published.

Lord Franks and his inquiry into the Falklands War of 1982 was equally non-judgemental. Lord F uncovered some pretty hard evidence about the government's failure to protect the Islands, but then came to some very soft conclusions. 'We would not be justified in attaching any criticism or blame to the present government … for the invasion of the Falkland Islands,' he wrote. This led ex-Prime Minister James Callaghan to comment in 1983: 'For 338 paragraphs he painted a splendid picture … [but] when Franks got to paragraph 339 he got fed up with the canvas he was painting, and chucked a bucket of whitewash over it.'

And ditto Lord Scott, who in 1996 came up with an eye-goggling 1,800-page report on the 'Arms to Iraq' scandal. Only 2 million words, M'lud? That'll do nicely. Amazingly, however, there were no conclusions at all in Lord Scott's report. There wasn't any room.

So here's a conclusion from this lack of conclusions: judges just don't seem to see it as part of their duty to judge governments. And governments know it. But you never know, things may be about to change, which is why we have the inquiry into inquiries.

It's easy to take the piss out of politicians for holding an inquiry into inquiries. But to be fair to them, they are at least responding to our growing cynicism about the way governments are churning these inquiries out. The politicians are effectively saying, 'OK, maybe we had better do something, or the public just won't take inquiries seriously any more.' As I mentioned earlier, I actually attended a meeting of the inquiry into inquiries at the House of Commons, when I started researching this book – a meeting at which Lord Howe, the dead sheep savager, and Lord Phil, the expert on the history of democracy, gave evidence. God it was boring. But it was also important. They were talking about the possibility of changing the rules, so that it wasn't just the PM choosing the chair of the inquiry; and they discussed maybe having three judges in charge, instead of one. If any of those suggestions gets taken up, then things might well be different next time – though somehow I doubt it. And anyway, if they did recommend changing the way inquiries are carried out, that would call for... another inquiry, surely?

One good thing about inquiries though: they're fantastic at showing us the bits of government that we never usually get to see. Hutton may have had his critics, but even they drooled over the amount and quality of the evidence that he collected. He also got brownie points for bunging the whole lot on the internet, where everyone could see it. His conclusions might not have been great for democracy – but his methods were.

CHAPTER TEN

Shooting Where the Ducks are: How to Get What You Want Without Voting

I don't know whether the last nine chapters have made you more, or less, keen to vote, but in my case I think it's the latter. Right now, voting doesn't really make a difference. It might bring in new names and faces, but the policies and attitudes stay pretty much the same. The new boss is pretty much the same as the old boss, as The Who noted in 1971 on 'Won't Get Fooled Again'. God, I love that song.

But I am, at least, a thinking non-voter. Last time out, in 2001, I didn't vote because there didn't seem to be much point. Like a game of rugby between the All Blacks and Papua New Guinea, I knew what the result was going to be beforehand. I was also very busy that day, interviewing a glamorous soap star about smoking for *Tonight with Trevor MacDonald*. So I couldn't actually make it to the Northcote Road polling station in Wandsworth, even if I'd wanted to. Some say not voting is unacceptably lazy and a threat to democracy. No, it isn't. A total of 25,557,009 people put their ticks in the boxes that day. I don't think the future of democracy in this country would have been any more secure if it had been 25,557,010.

When you confess to not having voted, a caring, socially aware type who reads a big newspaper will say: 'You didn't vote? My God! How can you expect to change things if you don't even use your vote? People died in wars so you could vote, you know.' And so on. To which I would now reply: 'Go back to north London and stop being so righteous. I would love to change certain things, but I don't know if voting's the best way to do it. Since when did voting *really* change anything?' All of this begs the question: what *is* the best way to change something – the parking system in your street, the state of your local hospital, Apartheid, or whatever?

One important rule is that you should 'shoot where the ducks are'. This is a phrase dreamed up by a clever American. It means you need to operate in the area where you will be most effective. It is the opposite of throwing loads of mud against the wall and seeing if any sticks. So if it's something to do with your local school, don't waste your time complaining to your local MP, but aim your initial fire at the people who control education in your area, ie the local council. Obvious, really. But you don't have to limit yourself to shooting at ducks if you don't want to: there are many other ways of bringing about change. Here is a list of options.

KILL YOURSELF

Apart from the obvious drawbacks, this has some merit. In 1913 Emily Davidson, who was campaigning for women to be allowed to vote, jumped in front of the King's horse, Anmer, as it was steaming towards the finishing line at the Derby. Horse and jockey survived; Emily didn't. Until that moment, women had been trying for 62 years to get the vote. They got it five years later. In fact, had WWI not happened in 1914, they might have got it sooner. It has always been assumed that Emily committed suicide, but the evidence suggests otherwise, as: a) she left no suicide note; b) she had already pencilled in the results of earlier races on her race card, which is not the behaviour of someone about to do themselves in; and c) tellingly, that morning, she had bought a *return* ticket to London.

Others argue that Emily's death was wasted. A more compelling reason for the Suffragettes' success, they say, was the fact that they downed their feminist tools in 1914 and supported the war effort.

Political brainboxes have a phrase for this option, which also covers suicide bombers, people who set themselves on fire and hunger strikers. It's called 'high-cost participation'. (You don't say.) Its effectiveness depends on a number of factors, the main one being the achievability of the aim. For example, al-Qaida's ambition – the destruction of Western civilisation and all it stands for – isn't that realistic. However, if it's a new playground for the primary school you're after, you could be in luck. After that it's simply of case of loading up the gun/tying the noose/filling up the petrol can and then weighing up the pros and cons.

WRITE TO YOUR LOCAL MP

Unless you are the victim of a gross miscarriage of justice or have been taken hostage by Peruvian mountain bandits, this could be a complete waste of time. Someone I know once worked as a dogsbody for five MPs in the space of one year. In that time he was on the receiving end of approximately ten thousand letters.

To the best of his knowledge, not one got a result. In fact, an awful lot ended up in the bin.

Where an MP can sometimes help, however, is when you're in a queue for hospital treatment, you want a pelican crossing near your school, your local street needs resurfacing, or whatever. An MP's headed notepaper can get you a result in these circumstances, because ministers and Town Hall bosses hate pesky backbench MPs and will sometimes throw them titbits to keep their noses out of serious policy-making.

But we shouldn't blame MPs too much: as we've seen, most are powerless individuals, and so, by definition, powerless to help. And to be fair, a lot of letters they get are from people complaining about being followed by orange dwarves from MI6. Many are simply unrealistic: asking your MP to bring about the downfall of a murderous foreign regime is like asking your telephone repair man to stop BT charging you so much. And writing to tell your MP that your local school/hospital/train service is crap, is good only for chest-clearance purposes. It is not shooting where the ducks are.

Even good old-fashioned blackmail – 'If you vote to invade Iraq, I will never vote for you again' – won't work: the MP's loyalty is always going to be to the party, not you. And if the party tells them there will be no jam for tea unless they vote to invade Iraq, they will vote to invade Iraq. If you must write, expect a pre-written letter in return, as in: 'Dear Mr Jones. Your local MP takes this issue very seriously. However, on this occasion...'

On rare occasions however, a conscientious MP will take up the cudgels on your behalf and write a letter to the relevant minister, who is then obliged to 'deal with the matter'. The minister — or rather, the minister's office — then *has* to do something: they are obliged to, by convention. This sounds encouraging, but usually isn't. For the minister, 'dealing with the matter' simply means officially acknowledging that the letter has been received. And so the end result is still the same, ie you get nowhere. In this case, though, you do at least get a slightly better quality of failure.

The very best thing you can hope for, realistically, is for your MP to act like a traffic policeman: they will occasionally point you in the right direction, but they will almost certainly not be able to get you there.

TRY TO BECOME AN MP YOURSELF

Ken Livingstone, the Mayor of London, once said that anyone seriously wanting to pursue a career in the House of Commons was almost certainly in need of immediate psychiatric help. That might not put you off. But the figures could: this option is time-consuming, expensive and almost certainly doomed to failure. In the last 70 years, only 11 independent candidates have been made MPs at a general election. So the odds of you getting in are about 6,000-1.

To stand as a candidate — you need to be over 21, and none of the following:

1. a peer in the House of Lords
2. a bishop
3. an undischarged bankrupt
4. a judge
5. a civil servant
6. in the armed forces or police
7. in jail

Interestingly, there is a centuries-old law that prevents "idiots" from standing for election. Unfortunately, this has yet to be tested in the courts. Moneywise, you will need to put down a £500 deposit, which you'll lose if you get less than 5 per cent of the vote. Rather unfairly, the deposit required for the European Parliament is £5,000: if you get less than 2.5 per cent of the total votes cast in the region, you lose the lot. That makes it virtually impossible for ordinary people – ie those not connected to big, well-funded parties – to stand.

You will be limited as to how much you can spend on your campaign, but that won't be a problem: it's £100,000. If you're interested, look at the website run by the Electoral Commission, the governing body of anything to do with voting (www.electoralcommission.gov.uk) for further details.

Mind you, even if you're successful and get in, there's no guarantee that you'll get what you want. Take Dr Richard Taylor, who played the 'Trust me, I'm a doctor' card in the Wyre Forest constituency in 2001. He stood for two reasons: to prevent the downgrading of his local hospital, and to re-open its A&E department. The balding, bespectacled 66-year-old doc single-handedly blew the big boys away. He won by a majority of 17,000 votes. The following morning, he was ecstatic. 'I think the most staggering thing is that the Chief Executive of the local health trust and one of its most important directors have shaken my hand,' he said. 'I've been persona non grata for three years and already they are looking to talk to me.' Sadly for him, that was as good as it got. The hospital stayed downgraded and the A&E department remained closed. The poor guy has spent four years of his life wandering the corridors of the Palace of Westminster in the knowledge that he had failed to achieve the very things he was elected to deliver. That's politics, Brian. Still, he made a point I suppose. And he got those two all-important handshakes.

However, if the issue that burns a hole in your belly is a national one, and you suspect that there are several other people around the country who feel like you, then you could always...

START YOUR OWN POLITICAL PARTY

Once upon a time there was a rabid anti-European called Dr Alan Sked, who wanted the Tory government to pull us out of the EU. He'd joined an organisation called the Bruges Group to try and make that happen, but without success. In 1991, he decided he'd have a better chance if he started his own party. He called it the 'Anti-Federalist League' and – good tip, this –

announced what he was doing in the letters page of *The Times*. Much to his surprise, he immediately got dozens of letters from people wanting to join, and quite a few donations (£50 here, £100 there, that sort of thing). When he decided to stand in the 1992 general election in Bath – which, at the time, was Tory bigwig Chris Patten's constituency – the press got very excited indeed. BBC2's *Newsnight* did a report on him. More letters, more donations. He took a bath in Bath, but the party carried on growing anyway. He told me: 'After a while, I felt like Doctor Frankenstein. I'd created a monster, and I didn't have any control over it.'

In 1997, Dr Sked had had enough, and left. The party then changed its name to the United Kingdom Independence Party (UKIP) and, despite Dr Sked's belief that it's now a refuge for dimwits and lunatics, it got more than 2 million votes in the European Elections of 2004. Dr Sked hasn't achieved his aim, of course. He has left a small but significant thumbprint on British political history, though: he helped light the anti-European fuse.

Pardon me while I go into *Blue Peter* mode, but if you want to start your own political party, all you will need is £150, and two people: a party leader and a treasurer. If you go to the Electoral Commission's website, you can download the application form. All the rules are there, including the ones about donations: anything over £200 has to be declared.

PUT A SPANNER IN THE BUREAUCRATIC WORKS (AKA THE McBROOM METHOD)

This is a good one. In early 2004, councillors in Durness in Scotland felt cars were whizzing through their town too quickly, and wanted speed restrictions. But first, by law, they had to advertise their intentions in the local papers to see if anybody objected. Initially, no one did. Then, at the eleventh hour, they got a letter from a Mr McBroom. He demanded an inquiry and said he wanted to give evidence. The council were then legally bound to set one up. On the appointed day an impressive collection of local bigwigs turned up at the town hall, as did a lorry load of journalists, all eager to see Mr McBroom in action. But he failed to show. Cue much head scratching and detective work.

It emerged that Mr McBroom was not, as was first thought, a local resident, but from York, 480 miles away. He had almost certainly never been to Durness in his life. He had found out about the council's policy on the internet, and set to work from his front room, with only a bottle of ginger beer and a packet of pork scratchings for company. In the end though, the speed restrictions went ahead. His only achievement was to inconvenience the local council, mightily. His activities weren't confined to Durness, mind you. It transpired that Mr McBroom had pulled off similar stunts in towns and cities all over Britain.

The beauty of the McBroom method is that it's cheap, involves virtually no physical effort whatsoever, and is a canny and completely lawful way of frustrating and

171

annoying people whose policies you don't agree with. The disadvantage is that rather like the speed bumps Mr McBroom seems to hate so much, it doesn't stop things altogether, it just slows them down. It's shooting where the ducks are, for sure. But it's only ruffling their feathers.

A much more sophisticated – and successful – version of this method was used by a bloke called Christopher Bailey. The events in question happened more than 25 years ago, but the story's a corker. It shows that with determination, money and good lawyers, one man can take on an entire government and win.

Mr Bailey owned a small ship-repairing company in South Wales. The Labour government wanted to nationalise it, and had drawn up a Bill to that effect. Mr Bailey was facing a forced sale of his life's work. He didn't fancy that, so he got his lawyers to examine the Bill line by line. They found a small, and not very serious, procedural defect. This held the Bill up for a bit. Mr Bailey told the government, politely, that if they carried on with the Bill, he would find more technical problems (ie 'There'll be more where that came from, sonny'). They ignored him. So he unleashed his legal dogs of war once more. Sure enough, they found several more small defects. The government realised they were only going to get their Bill through Parliament by giving in to Mr Bailey. So they did. They dropped the bit that referred to ship-repair companies. Game, set and match to Mr Bailey! This is duck shooting of the highest order and is really most impressive.

START A CONSUMER BOYCOTT

Lil and Tom live in north London and refuse to eat KitKats or drink Nescafé. They won't let their kids do it either. The reason for this is that both products are made by the giant Nestlé company, who sell a lot of baby milk powder to poor African families. Nestlé, it's argued, are causing babies to die. In some countries their powder might have to be mixed with unfiltered water, which can carry disease. Campaigners claim a child fed with powdered milk is 25 times more likely to die as a result of diarrhoea than a breast-fed one. An awful lot of people agree with Lil and Tom, which is why Nestlé are currently Public Enemy Number One when it comes to consumer boycotts.

The disadvantage of this method, as Tom points out, is that it is a very blunt instrument, as it comes with the following problems:

a) Nestlé make so many things it's hard to keep track, and so it's sometimes difficult to avoid consuming one of their products. A tempting meal of Buitoni pasta, washed down with Vittel mineral water, followed by a Maxibon ice cream, might seem innocent enough to your average Nestlé hater. But such a combo would be Lil and Tom's worst nightmare: all three items are in fact made by companies owned by Nestlé. The trouble for Lil and Tom, as Michael Caine would say, is that not many people know that.

173

b) Nestlé aren't the only company involved in selling the milk powder. There are shipping, packaging and distribution companies who, in the eyes of the protestors, have equal moral guilt, but they will escape the flak as they are too far down the food chain, as it were, and can't be got at by everyday shoppers.

c) There may be other chocolate bars nestling (sorry) right next door to the KitKats on the supermarket shelves, made by equally guilty companies, but they too will escape the flak. This is because it's difficult to target two companies at once for the same thing. Consumer boycotts work best when there is just one target.

The advantage of this method is that if enough people do it, it can have some effect. Companies like Nestlé think with their wallets: once they realise their profits are being eaten into and their KitKats aren't, they will sit up and listen, pronto. A spectacular example of this occurred in 1995, when Shell wanted to dismantle its massive, and very dirty, Brent Spar oil rig and dump it in the sea. Tree huggers everywhere were outraged, demanding they do it on land, instead of fouling up the oceans. Loads of people boycotted Shell garages and sales fell by up to 50 per cent. Shell backed down and instead spent £43 million on getting rid of the rig in a much 'greener' way. But, as I say, this instrument can be a bit blunt and is often more effective when combined with another form of protest. For example, chucking bombs (see below).

START YOUR OWN PRESSURE GROUP

There are a lot of angry parents in Brixton, south London, at the moment. Such as Devon Allison. (And no, I haven't got her name back to front.) Devon wants her young children to be educated locally and for free. Not unreasonable, given that she pays more than £1,000 a year in council tax to Lambeth to provide precisely that. But there are no secondary schools in Brixton. Yes, you read that right. Despite receiving over £90 million in council tax a year from local residents, Lambeth Council has no secondary schools in the biggest and most densely populated part of its borough. There were some – once – but they sold them all off to developers, who converted them into luxury flats.

So Devon and her mates decided to start a pressure group, to make Lambeth Council and the Department for Education build a decent local school. More and more people are doing this. Why? Because staffing a pressure group is more effective – and more direct – than voting, that's why. In the last 30 years, turnouts at election have fallen faster than Sven Goran Eriksson's trousers, while the number of pressure groups has gone into outer space. There used to be hundreds, but now, if you include charities – many of which could be described as pressure groups – there are more than 50,000.

Some pressure groups can be massive – The Confederation of British Industry (CBI), for example, represents 150,000 businesses – whereas SSCIL, Devon's lot (it stands for Secondary Schools Campaign In Lambeth) has around only 800 families.

Ironically, the most successful pressure groups always die: after all, once they've achieved their aims, what's the point in carrying on? Take possibly the first ever pressure group in history, the Society for Effecting the Abolition of the Slave Trade, which William Wilberforce founded in 1787. Twenty years later, happily, he found himself out of a job – and a pressure group – when slavery was indeed made illegal. The same thing happened to the Anti-Poll Tax Federation and a group with similar aims called Scrappit!

SSCIL, however, is still very much with us – though they hope to be dead soon. They've certainly made progress. Five years ago, they were told there was no way they'd get a secondary school built in Brixton. But now, land has been earmarked for development and the government has pledged enough money to build not one but two schools.

I thought a basic ten-point plan for people setting up pressure groups, big and small, might help. So here goes:

1. Think of a catchy name, like UNCLE or SMERSH. SSCIL isn't a good example,

obviously. But at least you can say it in one syllable.

2. Organise a meeting for like-minded people by handing out flyers in all the right places. In SSCIL's case this was the school gates. Or do what Alan Sked did, and write to a newspaper announcing what you've done. With a bit of luck, like him, you'll get not only letters of support, but dosh.

3. Bone up on the bizarre and complex ways of government and local government. You need to be able to talk their language, so in Devon's case that meant knowing what things like 'Band G capped budget allocations' were.

4. Don't be aggressive. Work *with* them, not against them. 'Don't piss them off, engage with them,' says Devon. It's not about saying, 'We're right, you're wrong,' it's about – politician speak coming up – moving forward together. In SSCIL's case that involved the parents actually going out and finding an area of land in Brixton where a school could be built. In other words, they did their leaders' jobs for them. It worked: the Government promised to give them £60 million.

5. When the way ahead gets blocked, as it surely will, use the media. They love any story that features battling ordinary people. But be careful how you go about attracting coverage

(see Publicity Stunts, below). If you go too far, you might piss people off and lose public sympathy. In SSCIL's case they go for harmless but clever photo opportunities, ie getting their kids to collect signatures for petitions.

6. For God's sake don't give up – just hang on in there and be patient. 'It's like a four-year-long game of chess,' says Devon.

7. If you've got money, you can actually pay an MP to put your case to Parliament. The MP will then be called your 'parliamentary adviser', and will have to declare the link in the Register of Members Interests. If your group is broke, but the MP is a good egg with principles, then he/she might do it for free. Pressure groups can also 'reward' MPs friendly to their cause by helping with their election campaigns. This sort of thing is going out of style, however. These days, many MPs won't touch it.

8. When you're well established and know your onions, you might be able to help frame new laws on your subject. Some pressure groups actually have bills written and ready to go, in the hope that one day, they might be needed. The Society for the Protection of the Unborn Child, for example, came up with several proposals for the Abortion (Amendment) Act. As it happens, the Act never got passed: it was – er – aborted.

9. You could try standing for Parliament. Pressure groups don't usually do this – they're usually defined as organisations that seek to influence government policy – but having said that, in the 1997 election there were more than 50 pressure-group candidates, including the Pro-Life Alliance and the Legalise Cannabis Campaign. Fathers 4 Justice are also planning to go down this route at the next general election. If all else fails, you could always try…

10. Violence. (See later on for further details.)

TAKE OVER YOUR LOCAL COUNCIL

I asked Devon why she and her fellow parents hadn't tried this one. If they had, and been successful, they could have built schools on every corner of every street. Devon said she'd considered this, but reckoned it would have been too time-consuming: she wanted to have a life.

There was also the duck issue. 'There were ducks at local council level, but also at government level,' she said. 'And to be honest, the biggest, juiciest ducks were at national level. This way, we can aim at both sets of ducks, without lots of other birds wandering in front of our target.'

Carole Karp, on the other hand, went for it. She lives in the district of Elmbridge, a place so posh even the tramps wear ties. The area covers some of the richest towns in Britain, such as Esher, Cobham, Weybridge and Oxshott. Despite bringing up five children and running a private medical practice in Harley Street, Carole managed to find time to take part in a kind of upmarket Peasants Revolt. It worked. After a long struggle – a lot of balsamic vinegar was spilled – the people of Elmbridge took over their local council.

Not that the people of Elmbridge weren't always running their local council, you understand. It's just that before Carole and her chums came on the scene, the council had been run by fully paid-up members of the Conservative Party.

'It wasn't that they didn't care about the place,' Carole says, 'but a lot of them had the wrong priorities – they were politicians and Tories first, and local residents second. They seemed to be coming at things from a different angle from the rest of us.'

As a result, says Carole, bad decisions were made. Horrible, environmentally unfriendly buildings were put up. The builders and the developers did well out of it, but local residents were infuriated. Then the council announced it was going to close six day-care centres for the elderly. More than a thousand local oldies were about to lose something that had been part of their daily routines for years: no more meals on wheels, no more Scrabble, no more tea dances. So Carole and a load of other residents stood for election, got in, and stopped the closures happening. The Scrabble and lemon curd sandwiches continue to this day.

The Stockbrokers' Revolt didn't stop there: in the year 2000, the local residents finally managed to take complete control of Elmbridge District Council. They must be doing something right, because they've kept power ever since. The whole process took a long time, mind you. The first local resident crept on to the council in the 1970s, and the power base expanded slowly after that.

The best thing about ordinary people running their own councils, says Carole, is that they don't have divided loyalties. All they care about is what's good for the area. Like the village shop in *The League of Gentlemen*: a local party for local people.

If a council is controlled by established, mainstream parties such as the Conservatives/Labour/Lib Dems, there may well be career politicians involved – ie people who are always looking over their shoulders, trying to impress their masters at National HQ. And what's in the best interests of the Conservative Party nationally, say, may not always be what's best for the locals.

Another good thing, says Carole, is that you are truly independent: you make up your own mind on each issue. The established parties, on the other hand, have whips, whose job it is to tell everyone exactly how they should vote. This leads to strange, undemocratic behaviour. 'Only one Tory of 50, say, might want something to happen, but then they'll all vote for it, whether they agree with it or not,' says Carole. 'It's bizarre. All their hands shoot up into the air, en masse, even though you know half of them don't like what's going on.' Carole and co., however, can vote any way they like, according to their consciences. Maybe I'm being naïve, but this seems more much sensible – and democratic. This kind of approach might not work at a national level – not yet, anyway – but it seems to have worked a treat in leafy, comfortable Elmbridge.

Strangely, though, there have been very few examples of the lunatics taking over the asylum, as it were. Only 12 out of 400 locals councils in England and Wales are currently controlled by ordinary people, ie independents. If you fancy changing that, it's pretty easy to set the ball rolling. Ring your local council, ask for the elections office, and get some application forms sent to you. But be prepared for the ball to be in play for a very long time – perhaps 20 years or more. So: go back to your kitchens and garden sheds and prepare for government. But be patient.

The beauty of this option is that even if you fail dismally at the ballot box, there's still a chance you will get exactly what you want. This is what happened in south-east London a few years ago. This remarkable story started in 1985, when the mighty Charlton Athletic Football Club were forced to leave their home ground, The Valley, after 66 years. Tears were shed. One night, a handful of fans met in a Bexleyheath pub and decided to put pressure on Greenwich Council to help the club return home. But the council wouldn't play ball.

Several years went by. The Valley became overgrown with weeds, gypsies moved in and a flock of kestrels began nesting in the disused floodlights. Eventually, after another failed attempt to get the council to grant planning permission to rebuild the stadium, the fans took matters into their owns hands. They formed The Valley Party, with the intention of standing in the local council elections of 1991.

Politics, like football, is a team game and that's exactly how The Valley Party played it. One of the fans was in advertising, so he handled publicity. (One poster featured a picture of legendary Charlton keeper Sam Bartram diving for the ball, with the caption: 'Sam can't save Charlton this time: but you can.')

Another fan was a journalist, so he took care of the press. A civil servant looked after the admin and the politics, and so on. Charlton fan Michael Grade, then controller of Channel 4, now BBC Chairman, also gave the campaign his blessing.

It worked, gloriously – but not in the way the fans had expected. Although The Valley Party managed to win an impressive 15,000 votes – a 10 per cent share – they failed to win a single seat on Greenwich Council. But they took a lot of votes away from the established parties. One consequence of this was that the Labour Chair of the Council's Planning Committee lost his seat. He burst into tears when the result was announced. His replacement, faced with such an impressive show of democratic solidarity, decided to back the fans. Eighteen months later, Charlton were back at The Valley.

In this case, nothing succeeded like failure. The club are now in the Premiership, and sell out every match they play. All together now: ahhh!

ORGANISE A DEMONSTRATION OR RALLY

This will get you on the news, if enough of you do it, but it doesn't score very well on the Duck Shooting Index. Take the mass Stop The War rally that took place in 2002, before the invasion of Iraq. It failed to stop the war. OK, it led the news bulletins and got in the papers. But it was shooting nowhere near the target: the rally took place in central London, but the ducks were 3,663 miles away in Washington.

LOB A FEW BOMBS

This can work if you have clear, well-defined, realistic aims and are willing to kill and maim in order to achieve them. British politicians might not like to admit it, but this tactic got results for the Provisional IRA. They started a campaign of violence in 1969. Less than 30 years later, the Good Friday Agreement was signed, which gave them much of what they wanted: Sinn Fein, the political wing of the IRA, got some very big seats at the table in the new Northern Ireland Assembly. It didn't do the African National Congress (ANC) much harm in South Africa, either. One day they were chucking bombs, the next they were running the county.

Then there's East Timor. A guerrilla group – FRETILIN – began a violent fight for independence after Indonesia invaded in 1975. Twenty-seven years later, the leader of FRETILIN, Xanana Gusmao, was chosen by a huge majority in presidential elections to be the country's first head of state.

All of this raises an important issue: what are you, exactly? Freedom fighters or terrorists? Ah, that old chestnut. Distinguishing between the two is difficult, but as a rule, terrorists generally kill more civilians than freedom fighters, who tend to concentrate on so-called 'legitimate targets', ie the armed forces and politicians. This is such a thorny subject that some broadcasters, like the BBC, simply avoid the issue altogether by using neither description. They refer to Palestinian suicide bombers, for example, as just that, so as not to cause offence.

If killing's not your bag, though, you could always…

START A RIOT

This worked a treat for the poll tax protestors in 1990.

Within months, the object of their hatred had gone. Some say it wasn't the violence itself that did the trick, but the instinct for self-preservation felt by Tory MPs, who realised that if the tax didn't go, they would: at the next election. In other words, the riots weren't, on their own, enough to get rid of the poll tax. But then again there's nothing like a big, televised ruck in central London to make those in power sit up, take note and realise they have a very serious problem on their hands.

PUBLICITY STUNTS

Scaling a crane in central London dressed as Spiderman, or standing on a ledge in front of Buckingham Palace togged up as Batman, gets you plenty of coverage in the media, but does it actually *achieve* anything? These were just two of the stunts carried out by the pressure group Fathers 4 Justice in 2004. They are campaigning for divorced fathers to be given the same rights as mothers when it comes to seeing their children.

There's one school of thought that says this sort of thing can backfire. Who on earth is going to give these blokes equal rights, they argue, when they behave like that? But Matt O'Connor of Fathers 4 Justice says the stunts have worked gloriously: 'We only started this stuff 20 months ago. Before that, no one had heard of us, no one was writing about us, no one gave a toss. Now, we've got editorials in the *Sun* saying the law needs changing, the Tory Party have held a summit on the family, and the government have done a Green Paper on the subject. I reckon we'll get what we want in 18 months. But it takes time. It's like sawing away at a giant redwood with a hacksaw.'

Matt says he's taken a leaf out of Gandhi's book – the man who, successfully and peacefully, campaigned for India to be made independent from Britain. The first and most important rule, Gandhi said, should be 'to make the injustice visible'.

When deciding on your stunt, you need to think about three things:

1. Will it make good pictures? Think TV news bulletins and newspaper front pages here.
2. Will it make a good story? The Batman stunt scored highly on this, as it highlighted the issue of the Queen's security.
3. Is there an element of wit and/or creativity involved? GM foods protestors dressed up as giant vegetables, that kind of thing.
4. Is there an opportunity to use food or drink? For some campaigners, creativity = cookability. And with good reason. A politician being assaulted with a grocery item of some description guarantees next-day coverage in the press. John Prescott, memorably, had an egg chucked at him. Fathers 4 Justice pelted the PM with flour. And John Prescott (again) had an ice bucket full of water tipped over him by someone called Danbert Nobacon. All three

incidents made headline news. The next step, surely, is to combine all three of those ingredients – eggs, flour and water – in one stunt. Pancakes anyone?

If the answer to all these questions is yes, you could be in business. The danger, however, is that the issue raised by your protest will be considered more important than the thing you're campaigning for. With the Batman stunt, for example, the TV news bulletins concentrated on how rubbish the security was at Buckingham Palace, rather than Fathers 4 Justice and their aims.

GET A CELEB ON BOARD

The beauty of this is that the celebrity doesn't even have to believe in the cause you're fighting for. They might not give a toss about your school/charity/rare animal, but still plug it, big style, as long as it's good for their image. You probably think I'm being a cynical git. In which case, take note of what tabloid publicist Max Clifford once said. He admitted that he encouraged stars to: 'Do stuff for charities, even if they don't want to. If they do it because they genuinely care, that's a wonderful bonus, but sadly that's not usually the case.'

There are rules you might want to observe, though, and things worth taking into account:

1. Don't go asking just any old celebrity for the sake of it. It might backfire. UNICEF, the

international children's charity, hit on the idea of getting ex-Spice Girl Geri Halliwell to be their 'Goodwill Ambassador'. But when she was interviewed about the cause on TV there was much chewing of knuckles. It swiftly became apparent that Geri hadn't quite grasped the complexities of the subject.

2. They might be more trouble and expense than they're worth. One rock star will only travel first class and stay in five-star hotels, all expenses paid, on charity jaunts. A famous actress has the same demands and once cost her charity thousands of pounds after going bonkers on room service and long-distance phone calls. Some simply demand – and get – a whopping fee. Although it's not actually called that, obviously. It's known as an 'honorarium'.

3. They might go disastrously off message. Naomi Campbell was once splashed all over billboards and magazines in the 'I'd Rather Go Naked Than Wear Fur' campaign. She also appeared on TV as a spokeswoman for the campaign. But then soon after that she sauntered down a Milan catwalk, decked out in fur. Oops.

4. If your cause isn't that sexy, save your energy: you're highly unlikely to get a celeb on board. As a general rule, the following causes will usually attract a star of some description:

children, animals, cancer, the environment, drink and drugs. But if it's mental health, domestic violence or incontinence you're trying to raise money for, it's going to be tricky.

Then again, if the celebs do the job, and get the charity noticed or raise loads of cash for it, who cares? The charities certainly don't. As Maria Pedro, celebrity manager of the NSPCC, puts it, some celebrities are 'only interested in relaunching or repositioning their careers, or getting access to other celebrities. But just because someone's motivation is not altruistic, doesn't mean it can't work for us. We don't care, frankly.'

You can understand why. Look at another ex-Spice Girl who may or may not have a completely concrete understanding of the issues involved with every charity she promotes: Victoria Beckham. In 2003 she was splashed across two pages of the *Daily Mirror*, alongside starving children in Africa. It got the charity concerned invaluable national exposure. It would have cost them £50,000 to take out an advert that size. And the cost of the trip was more than repaid by the money raised, so shocked were the public at the sight of such malnutrition. (The children's, not Victoria's.)

The moral is this: celebs open doors. But once you've gone through the doorway, it's down to you, and your powers of persuasion, to actually change things.

'Ah yes, but what about Band Aid in 1984,' you might say. As no doubt many of you will remember, in that year a load of pop stars came together and raised money for famine victims in Africa via a charity record and, the following year, twin concerts in the US and UK. They were hoping for a million. By the time they'd finished, they'd made £150 million. It's hard to criticise something which saved lives, and inspired various charity fests like the BBC's Sport Relief, which raises around £10 million a year. But if you are the arsey, bitter and twisted bloke who sits in the corner of the pub scowling, you might point out that Band Aid was, as its name implies, a sticking plaster, and not a long-term solution. It didn't − because it couldn't − address the fundamental problem that was causing such misery, ie corrupt and useless government. In fact, if you were really obnoxious, you might argue that charities such as Band Aid only served to prop up such regimes, which ensured that the misery continued. But then again, lives were saved.

Bono, lead singer of U2, is a perfect example of what celebs can achieve. It's all about getting issues onto the agenda. Before he started campaigning for poorer countries to be let off their debts, few gave a toss. Then he got started. Because of who he was, some of the most powerful politicians in the world − such as George W. Bush − fancied being photographed with him, realising how good it would be for their image.

All of a sudden, newspapers all over the world had a story: Bono and The Prez. (Yes I know it's sad that they think a pic of a pop star and a politician is more of a story than starving kids in Africa, but that's the way it is.) An issue that previously didn't even merit a line was suddenly big news everywhere. It wasn't just PR for the sake of it, either: it worked. In September 2004, the Chancellor announced he was cutting Third World debt. The only loser in this, arguably, was Bono, whose CQ (Cred Quotient) must have suffered horribly after being pictured next to George W.

HELP WRITE THE LAWS YOURSELF

This is a corker. You can actually log on to websites, see what laws are currently being proposed, and bung in your three pennies' worth. What's more, they have to take your views into account, even if they ignore you in the end. I spoke to Jessica Litten, who used to work for the Department of Constitutional Affairs, about how it all works:

'We would put everything on our website, I mean everything … the exact wording of the Bills we were proposing, the names of every organisation we'd sent details to, deadlines for comments, the lot.'

Yes, but you probably threw Joe Public's comments in the bin, didn't you?

'God no. We had to read, record and think about every single word we got. From everyone. All the time.'

The problem, of course, is that not everyone has the ability to log on. But there's always your local library. The exciting thing – well, refreshing at least – is that it's all there, right now. If you don't believe me, try it yourself. You could be at the bottom of a garden in boring Chiswick, like I am now, and within 30 seconds, telling the Government what you think should be done about a long list of important issues.

This concept of a more open, accessible government is a New Labour invention, and it would be mean not to congratulate them for it. It looks and smells highly democratic.

In the last ten minutes, for example, I have logged on to the Department of Health website (www.dh.gov.uk) to poke my nose into the issue of fluoride being put in our water. I then popped over to Jessica Litten's old employers (www.dca.gov.uk), to see what they're planning to do with the adoption laws. Then it was time to visit the Department of the Environment website (www.defra.gov.uk), and see in detail their current proposals for the welfare of goats, turkeys and – how appropriate – ducks. When it comes to shooting them, this scores highly.

If you have a special interest and you want to see what's going on, it's dead easy. Find out which government department controls the issue, type its name into Google or Yahoo!, and go to its website. Click on the words 'Consultation papers' and you're away. Make law, not war!

★ ★ ★ ★ ★

The bottom line is this: if you have enough popular support, sane and achievable aims, and are very, very patient, you stand a good chance of getting what you want, or something like it. Tony Benn, the ancient ex-politician who has been there and done that, puts it this way: 'At first, they think you're mad. Then they think you're dangerous. Then they ignore you, sometimes for several years. Then they claim the idea as their own, and reckon it was theirs all along.'

Come to think of it, he's right. The Suffragettes (they had to wait nearly eighty years to achieve their aims) and the Anti-Apartheid brigade (fifty years) both fit into this category. Campaigners for new schools, fewer speed cameras and fewer ugly buildings, take note. And good luck.

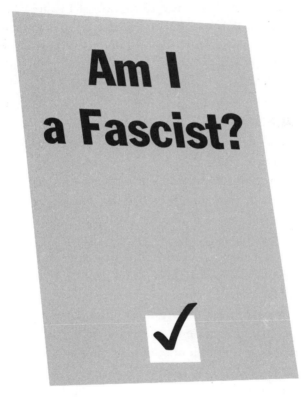

CHAPTER ELEVEN

Am I a Fascist?

I don't know. Mainly because I don't know what it means. It's a word I've heard slung around for years, along with 'communist', 'socialist', 'capitalist' and various other '-ists' and '-isms', but to be honest I've never had the nerve to admit that I hadn't a clue what any of them really involved. It's time to try and put that right, so here is my very rough guide to some popular political ideologies, past and present.

ANARCHISM

Anarchists don't believe in governments, or authority, of any kind. Their idea of the perfect society is one where everyone simply agrees to agree on everything. Ironic, given that anarchists can't even agree between themselves about how to achieve their aims. Some of them think the state should be overthrown peacefully; others want to use violence. The first English anarchist was a bloke called William Goodwin, who was born in 1756. He wanted everyone to behave as well as they possibly could. This, he argued, would mean there'd be no need for governments, so they'd eventually die out. Anarchism – the violent sort – reached its fashionable peak around 1900. Its leading light was a bloke called Johann Moser, who went round blowing up lots of things with dynamite. Anarchy lives on, though: a lot of those people you see throwing bombs and rioting at world trade summits and the like would describe themselves as anarchists.

In intellectual circles, the most famous anarchist round

today is called Noam Chomsky. His particular brand of anarchy involves the banning of property: he believes that nobody should 'own' anything.

CAPITALISM

... is the winner – currently, anyway – in the battle of the big economic '-isms' of the 20th century. It describes an economic system that is based on the making of profits. Capitalism's big idea is that you should be able to earn a reward, ie a profit, for putting your capital at risk in some form of economic activity.

Capitalism varies hugely, however, from one country to another. This is because they all disagree over the part that the state should play in the economy – ie a lot, or a little.

Karl Marx, inventor of another mighty '-ism' – communism – reckoned capitalism would never last. He said that it contained the seeds of its own destruction. The rich would get so rich, he reckoned, that the poor would rise up and kick them out and replace the whole shooting match with communism. He was wrong: his own baby kicked the bucket first.

People argue about when capitalism was invented. Some say it started when the feudal lords of England kicked poor peasants off their land and gave them small, enclosed spaces to work and live on. Others say it began with the slave trade. And a few say the Industrial Revolution was when it really got going.

A capitalist society will usually have the following characteristics:

1. A stock market.
2. An enormous amount of difference between the highest- and lowest-paid members of the society. (Take the UK: £10 million a year and £500 a year, respectively.)
3. A number of large organisations – ie businesses – who employ huge numbers of people and whose never-ending aim is to make more profit than they did the year before.

Here endeth the lesson.

COMMUNISM

Hasn't really caught on. In fact, it has been responsible, it is said, for the deaths of up to 50 million people. As the name suggests, communism means that everything – land, boats, houses, factories, etc. – should be owned communally, and not by families or individuals. In legal terms, property and ownership doesn't exist. So you can forget mortgages, for a start.

When it comes to divvying up the goodies in a communist society, there are two crucial things to take into account: ability and need. As Karl Marx, author of *Das Kapital* and the father of modern communism, put it: '*From* each, according to his abilities. *To* each according to his needs.'

In the perfect communist society, there's no class system. In theory, anyway. There isn't a government, either. One party – known, not surprisingly, as 'The

Party' – should control everything: politics, economics, culture, the lot.

As I said, that's the theory. In practice, many communist regimes have, according to observers in the West, been hopelessly bureaucratic, inefficient and corrupt. Not to mention repressive, secretive, cruel and abusive of human rights. Oh yes, and they don't work, either.

Cows are quite useful when it comes to explaining why. Pure communism, it is said, involves you sharing two cows with your neighbours. You and they bicker over who has the most ability and the most need. Meanwhile, no one works, no one gets any milk, and the cows drop dead of starvation.

Proper communism, according to Karl Marx, takes time to achieve. So he came up with 'socialism': the transition period that all societies have to go through before they can achieve the ultimate – full, perfect communism. This is why countries calling themselves 'socialist' have, confusingly, also been called 'communist' by us in the West – as in the (former) USSR: the United Socialist Soviet Republics.

Mind you, there aren't many examples of communism left: following the break-up of the Soviet Union (pub quizzers take note), only five communist societies remain: Vietnam, North Korea, Cuba and Laos.

That's only four countries, you may have noticed. The fifth deserves a paragraph all of its own, as it's a special case. When I said communism hasn't really worked, I was wrong, in a way. Why? China. The country practises a slightly diseased form of communism, as it's been infected with quite a lot of private enterprise since the early 1980s. But communist it definitely is: it's a one-party state, run by the Chinese Communist Party. It works too – big time – if economic prosperity, and not human rights, is your yardstick. China now has the fastest growing economy in the world.

There are various other strains of communism – Leninism, Trotskyism, hardline Marxism, Maoism, Stalinism and Bolshevism. Something tells me this is not the time, place, or book, to go into minute detail about what the theoretical and practical differences between them all are.

CONSERVATISM

If you're conservative, as opposed to a Conservative (ie a Tory), it's fair to say you believe in the following: capitalism, tradition, law and order, moral discipline and the impossibility of achieving anything like the perfect society dreamed up by, for example, Karl Marx. This is why it's often said that conservatism emphasises the 'politics of imperfection'. A lot of conservatives don't like anyone trying to define conservatism too closely because, they say, part of its appeal is that it is very adaptable. A true conservative, they argue, will change his or her mind and abandon a particular goal, to conserve (geddit?) the vital interests of society. In other words, it's not a doctrine, or a philosophy, it's a state of mind. If, however, you are a Conservative, you will generally believe in a) all of the above; b) low taxes, c) less government and d) whatever else you think will get you elected.

Conservatism has a (for some) rather frightening mother-in-law called 'neoconservatism' (see below).

FASCISM

... is pretty much dead, so we don't need to worry about it any more. Once, though, it was very much alive. The movement was formed in Italy in 1919, a time when there was a deep social and economic crisis. People were looking for something different, something that worked, and they believed fascism might be the answer. Success came quickly: Benito Mussolini led the fascists to power in Italy just three years after they'd formed, and they stayed there until 1945.

Fascists believe the state is everything, and that it should have total and absolute authority. As Mussolini put it, the state should 'govern and mould individual wills'. Unlike communism, it doesn't have a coherent system of ideas, however. Fascists weren't too hot on defining exactly what it was they liked. But they sure knew what they hated. And that was just about everything. They hated communism, democracy, the working class, trade unions, Jews, ethnic minorities and parliamentary parties. They thought there should be just the one party, preferably with a charismatic leader. (If this sounds familiar, you're right – Nazism was a form of fascism.) Fascism has a very military flavour: its followers believed in violence and war. There were lots of uniforms, ranks, salutes and rallies. Many fascist regimes, like those in places such as Belgium, Romania and Norway, got wiped out at the end of WWII. The most recent example of a fascist regime, it's argued, was the apartheid system in South Africa, which ended in 1994.

Other notable fascist regimes included Argentina (they had it for nine years after WWII and for a year in the 1970s), Spain (nearly forty years of it, under General Franco or 'El Caudillo' as he was known) and Portugal (a mild form of it, for forty years, till the mid-1970s).

Britain actually flirted with fascism a bit before WWII. A former Labour Party minister called Oswald Mosley formed the British Union of Fascists in 1932 and, at the height of his popularity, the party had 40,000 members. Then came the war and the British fascists – known as the 'black shirts', after their trademark attire – all got shunted off to the Isle of Man. Interestingly, the British fascists were the first political party in the UK to call for European integration. (They did so in 1949.)

ISLAMIC FUNDAMENTALISM

I know what you're thinking: Islam is a religion. What's it doing in a chapter on different political philosophies ? Well, for a kick-off, Islam is *the* biggest political issue, so far, of the 21st century: so I had to include it somewhere, didn't I?

And it's more than just a religion. It's a profound influence on laws and governments all over the world. It affects the way hundreds of million of people are ruled.

To put it another way, '*Islam din wa dawla.*' This is an Islamic mantra. It means 'Islam is religion *and* state.'

Islam is the fastest growing religion in the world, with over 1.2 billion followers. There are now Islamic influenced governments or laws in 46 countries throughout Africa, the Middle East and Asia. They include Thailand, Turkey, Algeria, Morocco, Indonesia, Saudi Arabia, Pakistan, Iran, Morocco and Malaysia.

There are several reasons for this astonishing rise. For one, the growing resentment at the huge wealth and power of the West – and of America in particular. Islam gives followers an alternative to the morally repellent ways (drug abuse, exploitation of sex, corruption, etc.) of the West. Then there's the political events that have helped to fan the flames: the Islamic-inspired Iranian Revolution of the late 1970s, for example. Bung all these factors into one big pot and it begins to make sense.

There is a problem, however. Islam and the West appear to be on a collision course. This is partly because Islam and democracy don't go very well together. We should briefly explore the reason for this. It has a lot to do with something called the Sharia. This is the body of Islamic law put together in the ninth century. It is the practical way in which Islam makes its presence felt in many countries. In many states, the Sharia is actually part of the law. But trying to run 21st-century lives according to ninth-century rules has, inevitably, led to problems.

Take Pakistan. Their interpretation of the Sharia is pretty radical. Thieves can have their right hands cut off.

Drinking alcohol can get you 80 lashes of the whip and the maximum punishment for adultery is death by stoning. But the law doesn't distinguish between women who have been raped and adulterers. This means that women who are raped often end up being severely punished: even killed. What's more, women are not allowed to give evidence on their own behalf.

But the good news – for fans of human rights, at any rate – is that things are changing. In several countries, hardline and intolerant interpretations of the Sharia are being challenged, and even shelved. In Pakistan, for example, popular protests against the inflexible interpretation of Sharia law are in full swing across the country. Something called the Joint Action Committee, which is leading the campaign, says the laws have 'not only given a bad name to our religion, but defamed Pakistan in the world'. It's working: the President of Pakistan has agreed to set up a special council to decide on the issue.

In Morocco, they've gone one better. King Mohammed VI recently introduced a revolutionary document: a new body of Islamic family law, which swept away centuries of bigotry and bias against women. As a result, women can now get married without needing the legal consent of a guardian. Men cannot verbally divorce their wives. Women are allowed alimony, and can get custody of their children. And so on. The crucial thing here, was that the religious scholars were totally onside. They were consulted, and cooperated, every step of the way.

As a result, the Islamist Party of Justice and Development in Morocco said it was a pioneering reform 'in line with the prescriptions of Islam, and with the aims of our religion'. Now that's what I call progress. Moral of the story: you've got to take them with you.

Finally, look at Malaysia. In the most recent election there, the PM, Mr Badawi, argued that Islam was far too associated with violence and extremism. It needed a re-think. So he invented a new concept: progressive, modern Islam, or 'Islam Hadhari' as he called it. This new form of Islam doesn't dwell on the past, but emphasises the present and the future. It also encourages wisdom, practicality, harmony and moderation. The good news? For the first time, his governing coalition won more than 90 per cent of the federal parliamentary seats. The hardliners were routed.

But not all followers of Islam want to go down this moderate, 'enlightened', modern route. There's still a small but sizeable minority of hardened Islamists who prefer the old ways of thinking. And some of them have turned to terrorism.

When I first came to this subject, being the moron I was, I lumped the issues of Islam and terrorism together. Which was unpardonably ignorant of me: it's the sort of thinking that once made people assume that if you were Irish and a Catholic, you must be an IRA terrorist.

But that's no reason to ignore the issue of Islamic terrorism. The fundamentalists who practise it may only be a tiny minority, but it's now – if you believe our leaders – the biggest threat to world security there is.

The big question is, what's caused it ? What turns a person from a law-abiding citizen into someone who is prepared to fly a plane into a tall building and kill thousands of innocent civilians? I must be careful here, obviously. I don't want to end up starring in my very own Al-Jazeera video. But here goes.

There are a number of factors. For the historically minded Islamists, there were scores to settle: the West had invaded, conquered and exploited Islamic regions for centuries. Then there was that disgust at the West's perceived lack of moral standards, described earlier. Palestine is also hugely important. When Israel was created in 1948, Palestinians lost their own country. This was seen by many Arabs as an appalling injustice. It fanned the flames of Islamic fundamentalism, big time. Also, if you're an unemployed, disaffected Muslim living in the West – a description that fits many Islamic terrorists – fundamentalism gives you the chance to feel special and unique. Muslim men, for example, believe that all those who kill themselves in the name of Islam will be rewarded in the afterlife with wall-to-wall virgins. Which obviously acts as quite an incentive.

These hardliners may be in the minority, but there are still plenty of them around. It's been estimated, scarily, that there are actually 18,000 al-Quaida 'operatives' scattered around the world, waiting to pounce. The war in Iraq, it's argued, has only made the problem worse. So what's to be done? Well, to use a well-worn phrase, we need to win over hearts and minds. Which is very difficult. But that's what we pay our politicians for, innit?

The bad news is that the leader of the most powerful country in the world – America – doesn't seem to have grasped the importance of this 'hearts and minds' business yet. In the eyes of the recently re-elected President Bush, it's a case of, 'You're either for us... or against us.'

But the good news – judging by the evidence of Malaysia, Pakistan and Morocco – is that with time, patience and tolerance, the threat of Islamic fundamentalism can be dealt with. Jaw jaw, not war war, as they say.

LIBERTARIANISM

People who believe in this throw good parties. The general idea is that anything goes. It is not the job of the state, libertarians argue, to decide how a person should behave. As long as your actions don't harm others, they argue, you should be allowed to do whatever you want. And that includes sexual perversion, drug taking and prostitution. Libertarians also think that government spending on things like defence, and the welfare state, is a complete waste of money. Not surprisingly, there have been very few libertarian governments. OK, none.

NEOCONSERVATISM

Seven syllables, one almighty argument: if you so much as mention the word neoconservatism around political types, retire swiftly, because you've lit the blue touchpaper.

The philosophy of neoconservatism was born in America in the 1960s and is nearly always used when people talk about America's foreign policy. But neocons, as they're known, believe in domestic policies too. Such as cutting taxes, pruning the welfare state and 'cracking down on vulgarity' – ie yobbish behaviour, pornography, etc. But that's not what's got the world talking about them.

Neocons came into their own after 9/11. Before that, they had been arguing for ages that the USA should get rid of Saddam Hussein, but without success. After 9/11, they won that particular argument, as you may have noticed. Because their views are so clear-cut and extreme, an awful lot's been said and written about them. Here's a quick checklist of what they stand for. Neocons believe that:

1. The USA should not be ashamed to use its unrivalled power, forcefully if necessary, to promote its values around the world.
2. The USA made big mistakes when President Clinton was in power by allowing dangers to fester, by not spending enough on defence and by not confronting threats aggressively enough.
3. The USA should stand by Israel come what may, as it's a beacon of democracy in a ocean of despotism – and if Israel wasn't there the Middle East would be even more volatile than it is already.

4. The Middle East should be 'democratised'. (They've already started on that one.)

5. The USA shouldn't pay too much attention to organisations such as the UN because they, unlike the neocons, don't know what's best for the world.

6. American patriotism is a wonderful thing and should be actively encouraged.

7. There's nothing wrong with identifying who your enemies are, in the clearest possible terms. President Reagan, neocons say, had exactly the right idea when he talked about the USSR as 'The Evil Empire'.

Many people are frightened and/or appalled by the neocons. They argue that invading Iraq was a ghastly, counterproductive mistake: it caused *more* terrorism, not less. They're also worried that with neocons in control at the White House, WWIII might not be too far away: the logical next step, they say, is for the USA to start making threatening noises to Iran and North Korea – which has a big fat nuclear bomb at its disposal.

But there's plenty of evidence to suggest that the power of the neocons has been exaggerated. (Not surprisingly, as it's a great story: 'Foaming Right-Wing Ranters Take Over White House'.) They don't actually dominate American politics: those in the know claim they just happened to win the individual argument over Iraq, that's all. And they're not planning to bomb the

crap out of Iran or North Korea any time soon: they'd much rather bring about democracy in those countries by other means, for example by supporting opposition groups. A military preemptive strike on these countries (eek! Stock up with baked beans and head for the cellar!) is only something that will happen as a last resort. There's the small matter of post-conflict Iraq to deal with first, anyway.

This idea of getting involved abroad is nothing new. Neocons argue they did it in WWII − when they bailed us Europeans out − and they've been doing it ever since, in Vietnam, Kosovo, Bosnia and so on.

Critics sneer that the Yanks want nothing less than to rule the world: an American Empire. To which neocons reply something along the lines of, 'Well hey, if that's what you want to call it, that's fine by us. If that's what's needed to make the world a safer place, who cares?'

Watch this space, as they say.

SOCIALISM

There are several different types of socialism. In its purest and most extreme form, a very controlling central government produces and distributes all the important goods, ie everything from food and property to water and electricity. In theory, because the government only wants what's best for its people, everything will get doled out fairly. In practice, however, many out-and-out socialist governments have ended up being dictatorships: the workers are ruled over, and exploited, by an elite. That's what happened in the USSR, for example, before President Gorbachev tried changing things in the late 1980s.

Then there's British-style socialism: a watered-down version of the hardcore variety. Strictly speaking, socialism, British style, should be called social democracy. As any political boffin will tell you, social democracy differes from pure socialism in one, crucial, respect: it don't need no revolution to get started. The basic aim of British social democracy has always been to try and make society more equal, by redistributing the dosh around. We've never really taken the ultimate socialist option of the government controlling and owning everything. We've gone down the mixed-economy route instead: a combination of socialism and capitalism. The socialist bit involved the government owning (up until the 1980s, anyway) large swathes of industry, keeping a tight rein on the economy and running a very generous welfare state system, ie pensions and benefits. The capitalist bit allowed room for lots of free enterprise and private money-making as well.

The Labour Party used to be a proper, copper-bottomed British style socialist party – but when Tony Blair took over in 1994, all that changed. The key moment was when he got the party to ditch Clause 4 of its 1918 constitution. The old Clause 4 committed Labour to public ownership. For many in the party, that was what made Labour Labour. Instead, the new Clause 4 offered a more wishy-washy commitment to social justice. This left the party free to raid the Tory cupboard for as many policies as they wished. For some hardcore Labour types, this was a betrayal of everything the party stood for, and they've never forgiven Tony Blair.

Dumping the old Clause 4 was what enabled Labour to add the 'New' to their name. It also meant Tony Blair could start going on about a so-called 'third way': ie one that was neither socialist nor capitalist, but a bit of both.

CHAPTER TWELVE

The (Quite) Democratic Index: How do They do it?

By 'they', I mean the rest of the world. Is Sierra Leone a democracy, or what? And how, exactly, do you define democracy, anyway? If you've ever asked yourself these questions, this is the chapter for you. It's a tell-their-political-colours-at-a-glance list of every single country in the world.

Unlike the last chapter, which was about political philosophies and isms, this bit is simply about how democratic every country in the world is (or isn't). Here's a guide to the definitions.

DEMOCRACY (DEM)

Has taken over the world. In 1900, there were no countries on earth with a full, unfettered democracy, ie where everyone had the vote, and the elections were free and fair and competitive. By 1999 however, 119 countries had universal adult suffrage. That's 62 per cent of the globe.

Democracies have to meet certain criteria, however, before they can be described as such:

The elections must be free. This means they must be held frequently, every citizen must have the right to vote, and the ballot should be in secret.

There must be a choice: if there's only one party to vote for, it ain't a democracy.

The elected representatives must have the right to pass laws and, if they wish, oppose government policy without being threatened/harassed/dragged off by hooded thugs in the dead of night.

RESTRICTED DEMOCRACY (RD)

… is to democracy what a veggie burger is to a hamburger: it might look a bit like the real thing, from a distance, but it isn't. Restricted democracies tend to have an overdominant ruling party controlling the levers of power. They keep a tight rein on the media, for example. And they don't allow free and fair elections that might challenge that dominance. Amusingly, countries that go in for this sort of thing prefer to call themselves 'guided democracies': they guide who you vote for. Clearly, they've missed the point a bit, but there we go. A typical example of a restricted (or, indeed, guided) democracy is Iran, where you can only run as a candidate if the religious authorities say so. And they have decided to ban, among others, the Green Party and the Communist Party. Some restricted democracies (Egypt for example), might *call* themselves democracies, but they're not.

By the way, if you're wondering what criteria I'm using for these assessments, most of the information in this chapter is gleaned from an American organisation called Freedom House, which is committed to the cause of democracy.

MONARCHY (MON)

The term originally meant 'the rule of one', but today it's used to describe a situation – no harm in stating the obvious, I always think – where supreme power (and wealth) is placed in the hands of a ruler, usually for life, and nearly always because they were born into it, the lucky sods.

217

AUTHORITARIAN (AUT)

States that practise authoritarian rule are, typically, those with just the one party – and an intolerant, meddling, repressive one at that. The ruler's powers are often limitless, and individuals have few rights, if any. Sometimes the party will, effectively, be the military. So, some of the countries I've listed as being authoritarian could also be called military dictatorships. Or, indeed, 'totalitarian'. Once upon a time, political cud chewers used to make a distinction between authoritarian and totalitarian. But we don't need to. They are, effectively, one and the same thing. Both political systems involve human rights violations, a large amount of control of most methods of communication, the (often violent) suppression of dissidence and regular intrusions into private life. Interestingly, the *Daily Mail* argues that if fox hunting gets banned in Britain, we will have become a totalitarian state. I think they are referring to the bit about intruding into our private life. Bit of an exaggeration, obviously, but I suppose they have a point.

★ ★ ★ ★ ★

OK, here are the countries. Things being what they are, some of the countries below might have changed their political colours in between me writing this and the book getting published. In which case, apologies.

Afghanistan
(DEM) But only just

The Taliban were in control here until 2001, but wouldn't, or couldn't, give up Osama bin Laden, so the Americans bombed the country into democracy, which is an interesting concept. The current head of state, Hamid Karzai, doesn't exactly rule the roost: his government exerts little control beyond the capital, Kabul.

Albania (DEM)

Algeria (AUT/RD)

Andorra (DEM)

Angola (AUT)

Antigua (RD)

Argentina (DEM)

Armenia (DEM)

Australia (DEM)

They may have given us various lagers, but we gave them democracy: the Aussie system is one of several around the world that is based on ours. They have, like us, two houses of parliament – theirs are called the Senate and the House of Representatives. The big difference, though, is that they have a strong federal element to their system. This means they have six separate states within the system, each with a good deal of power to control their own affairs. Our Queen is still their symbolic head of state – she is represented there by a governor general. The Aussies could have cut their ties with the monarchy in 1999, but voted not to.

Austria (DEM)

Azerbaijan (AUT)

Bahamas (DEM)

Bahrain (MON)

Bangladesh (DEM)

Barbados (DEM)

Belarus (AUT)

Belgium (DEM)

Belize (DEM)

Benin (DEM)

Bhutan (MON)

Bolivia (DEM)

Bosnia-Herzegovina (DEM)
Although technically, it's a
Prot, ie a protectorate.
After the Balkan conflict
from 1992–5, the Dayton
Peace Accord set up two
'entities': this one, and the
Serb Republic. Both have
their own government
and parliament but there
is also an overarching
central Bosnian
government.

Botswana (DEM)

Brazil (DEM)

Brunei (MON)

Bulgaria (DEM)

Burkina Faso (AUT)

Burma (AUT)
Go to the back of the
class, Burma. According
to a website that
monitors democracy
around the world,
www.worldaudit.org, you
are the least democractic
country on the planet.

Burundi (AUT)

Cambodia (RD)

Cameroon (RD)

Canada (DEM)

Cape Verde (DEM)

**Central African
Republic (DEM)**

Chad (RD)

Chile (DEM)

China (AUT)

That said, if you look closely, you'll find small specks of democracy on the Chinese underbelly. They have something called 'disapproval voting': the Chinese people can vote on whether newly elected party bigwigs are doing well. If the bigwigs don't get an 80 per cent approval rating at least, they usually don't go any higher. It's democracy, Jim, but not as we know it.

Colombia (DEM)

Comoros (RD)

Congo (AUT)

Costa Rica (DEM)

Côte d'Ivoire (AUT)

Croatia (DEM)

Cuba (AUT)

Fidel Castro has been in the box seat for 45 years, and he can't carry on for ever, obviously. When he goes, Cuba might become more **DEM** than **AUT** – especially if America has anything to do with it.

Cyprus (DEM)

The Czech Republic (DEM)

The Democratic Republic of the Congo (DEM)

Denmark (DEM)

Djibouti (DEM)

Dominica (DEM)

Dominican Republic (DEM)

East Timor (DEM)

Ecuador (DEM)

Egypt (RD)

The current president, Hosni Mubarak, leads the inappropriately named National Democratic Party, which has a reputation for crushing the democratic process. Egypt has an identity crisis. It's not sure whether to embrace Western modernity, or Islam, or try reconciling the two.

El Salvador (DEM)

Equatorial Guinea (AUT)

Eritrea (AUT)

Estonia (DEM)

Ethiopia (AUT)

Fiji (DEM)

Finland (DEM)

Not any old **DEM**, mind you. According to www.worldaudit.org, Finland is the most democratic country in the world. Meanwhile, out of the 149 countries listed, the UK comes a very respectable 10th.

France (DEM)

Theirs is what's known as a 'semi-presidential' democracy. That is, they have both a president and a prime minister. Their president is directly elected by the people: in French presidential elections, they vote for a person, not a party. Therefore, he has more of a – key phrase coming up – 'popular mandate', theoretically at least, than our PM, as millions of the electorate have personally voted for him. *Le President* usually controls foreign policy, while *le PM* and his *gouvernement* run the country. One monitors the other: that's the French system of checks and balances.

Gabon (AUT)

Gambia (AUT)

Georgia (DEM)

Germany (DEM)

Ghana (DEM)

Greece (DEM)

Grenada (DEM)

Guatemala (DEM)

Guinea (AUT)

Guyana (DEM)

Haiti (DEM)

Honduras (DEM)

Hungary (DEM)

Iceland (DEM)

India (DEM)

The world's biggest: 354 million voters, more than 500 parties and a mere 600,000 polling stations at the last election. The Indian system is based on ours: it's a combination of a written constitution from 1950, and bits of English common law, ie old customs. They have two houses of parliament: the Rayja Sabha, or upper house, and Lok Sabha, the lower house. There is a strong federal element here, too: there are 29 states, and six so-called 'union territories'.

Indonesia (DEM)

Iran (RD)
See above.

Iraq (WIP)
Work In Progress. Was an **AUT**, obviously, but currently trying to become a **DEM**. May end up as **HUNOTNTO**: Horrendously Unstable: Neither One Thing Nor The Other.

Ireland (DEM)

Israel (DEM)
Only one house of parliament, known as the Knesset. Came into being in 1948, when Israel was

created out of what was Palestine. It has 120 members. Israeli politics has never been dominated by one party: the current ruling government is typical in that it consists of four parties and has only a small majority.

Italy (DEM)

Jamaica (DEM)

Japan (DEM)

Jordan (RD/MON)

Kazakhstan (RD)

Kenya (RD)

Kiribati (DEM)

Korea, North (AUT)
This place is a prime candidate for prosecution under the Trades Descriptions Act. North Korea's official title is the 'Democratic People's Republic of Korea', yet this is one of the world's most secretive societies. North Korea emerged in 1948 out of the chaos at the end of WWII and its history has been dominated by its late Great Leader, Kim Il-Sung. His son, Kim Jong Il, is now in charge, but there's not much evidence that Sung's son is singing a different song. It's reckoned there are more than 200,000 political prisoners being kept here and the worry is that the North Koreans have a nuclear bomb and they might use it. President Bush, it's argued, made a delicate situation even worse by describing North Korea as part of a worldwide 'Axis of Evil'.

Korea, South (DEM)

Kuwait (MON/AUT)

Kyrgyz Republic (DEM)
Pity this country's name isn't allowed in Scrabble.

Laos (AUT)

Latvia (DEM)

Lebanon (TOT)

Lesotho (RD)

Liberia (DEM)

Libya (AUT)

Liechtenstein (DEM)

Lithuania (DEM)

Luxembourg (DEM)

Macedonia (DEM)

Madagascar (DEM)

Malawi (DEM)

Malaysia (RD)

Maldives (AUT)

Mali (DEM)

Malta (DEM)

Marshall Islands (DEM)

Mauritania (AUT)

Mauritius (AUT)

Mexico (RD)

Micronesia (DEM)

Moldova (DEM)

Monaco (DEM)

Mongolia (DEM)

Morocco (MON)

Mozambique (DEM)

Namibia (DEM)

Nauru (DEM)

Nepal (DEM)

The Netherlands (DEM)

New Zealand (DEM)

Nicaragua (DEM)

Niger (DEM)

Nigeria (DEM)

Norway (DEM)

Oman (MON)

Pakistan (AUT)

Palau (DEM)

Panama (DEM)

Papua New Guinea (DEM)

Paraguay (DEM)

Peru (AUT)

The Philippines (DEM)

Poland (DEM)

225

Portugal (DEM)

Qatar (MON)

Romania (DEM)

Russia (RD)

Under the 1993 constitution, the President has sweeping powers. Boris Yeltsin never made the most of these but the current president, Vladimir Putin, uses them to the max, and has even given himself new ones. The crisis with Chechnya has given him the opportunity to grab even more power. Russia's regional governors, for example, may no longer be elected, but appointed by him. Could soon be classified as an **AUT**.

Rwanda (AUT)

St Kitts and Nevis (DEM)

Saint Lucia (DEM)

Saint Vincent (DEM)

Samoa (DEM)

San Marino (DEM)

Sao Tome and Principe (DEM)

Saudi Arabia (MON)

The King is also the Prime Minister; political parties aren't allowed and the nearest thing they have to a parliament is a Council of Ministers, which can pass laws – if the King likes them, of course. The leadership's refusal to tolerate opposition, it's argued, may have encouraged the growth of dissident groups such as al–Qaida. Since then, the demands for greater democracy have got louder. But there is also a powerful Islamic presence in the country. Because of its position in the world, geographically and politically, Saudi Arabia is crucially important, which is why eyes are constantly on it.

Senegal (RD)

Serbia and Montenegro (AUT)
Not to be confused with the Serb Republic. See Bosnia-Herzegovina.

Seychelles (DEM)

Sierra Leone (DEM)

Singapore (AUT)

Slovakia (DEM)

Slovenia (DEM)

Solomon Islands (DEM)

Somalia (AUT)

South Africa (DEM)

Spain (DEM)

Sri Lanka (DEM)

Sudan (AUT)

Surinam (DEM)

Swaziland (MON)

Sweden (DEM)

Switzerland (DEM)

Syria (AUT)

Taiwan (RD)

Tajikistan (RD)

Tanzania (RD)

Thailand (DEM)

Togo (DEM)

Tonga (RD)

Trinidad and Tobago (DEM)

Tunisia (AUT)

Turkey (DEM)

Turkmenistan (AUT)

Tuvalu (DEM)

Uganda (AUT)

Ukraine (DEM)

United Arab Emirates (MON)

United Kingdom (DEM)
Or **AUT** if you believe the *Daily Mail*.

USA (DEM)
A full-blown presidential democracy: the federal kind, based on the written constitution of 1787. 'Federal', in this

227

case, means that there is a very powerful level of government below the national level. This means that the 50 states can set their own criminal and civil laws, and control things such as business and education. But the national government retains power over foreign affairs and defence. If you've never quite understood exactly what the Senate or House of Representatives do, or what Congress is, and what their relationship with each other is, don't worry, you're not alone – see next chapter, under 'C is for Congress'.

Uruguay (DEM)

Uzbekistan (AUT)

Vanuatu (DEM)

Venezuela (DEM)

Vietnam (AUT)

Yemen (RD)

Zambia (AUT)

Zimbabwe (RD – arguably AUT)

Robert Mugabe has been in power here since 1980. Back then he was a hero for getting rid of the whites-only government. But now he uses thugs to clamp down on free speech, the courts and opposition parties. He claims he is going to step down in 2008, in which case Zimbabwe might have a chance of becoming a **DEM**.

CHAPTER THIRTEEN

Quite a few
Useful Things
you Wanted to
Know about
Politics But were
Afraid to Ask
(From A to Z)

A IS FOR ADMINISTRATIVE ACTION

It may sound as exciting as a week-long accountancy seminar, but it gets government ministers very excited indeed.

Administrative Action (AA), along with something called 'Statutory Instruments' (SIs) are ways of getting big things done, *without* the pain and trauma of trying to steer a Bill through Parliament. (For an explanation of just how painful that process can be, see C is for Committee, below.) AA and SIs mean important things can be achieved miraculously quickly.

Administrative action entails a minister simply picking up the phone, having a chat, signing the relevant bit of paper, and bingo: £3 million goes to famine victims/a bypass is built/a train company loses its franchise.

'Statutory instruments' – sometimes known as Orders in Council, or 'secondary legislation' – are probably the most effective weapons in any minister's armoury. This is because, once they've been issued, they are every bit as much the law of the land as full-blown Acts of Parliament. Around 3,000 get passed every year. However, a minister can fire off a statutory instrument *only* if a relevant Act of Parliament gives him or her the power to: if it's reckoned a minister has gone one SI too far, Parliament can sometimes cancel it.

Ministers still dream of the ultimate political achievement: getting their own Bill through Parliament. But they soon wise up when they realise that shepherding a Bill through both Houses of Parliament takes more time and energy than pushing a Range Rover up a mountain. After which they tend to stick to the less glamorous, but more effective, AA and SIs.

B IS FOR BLACK ROD

Black Rod is Parliament's equivalent of the pantomime dame. He's not important politically; he is best known for carrying out a quaint, symbolic piece of parliamentary tradition. And wearing tights. (Although they're actually knee-length silk stockings.)

Black Rod's moment of glory is the historical ceremony for the State Opening of Parliament. He gets togged up in medieval gear (which explains the stockings) and 'summons' all MPs to the House of Lords, to hear the Queen's speech. During the ritual, as he approaches the House of Commons, the doors are slammed in his face. He strikes them three times with his rod. He is then asked a question – 'Who is there ?' – to which he replies 'Black Rod.' He is let in and invites all MPs to the Lords for the Queen's speech – which isn't, incidentally, written by her: it's the work of the government, a device to announce their plans for the next Parliament.

This whole scene starring Black Rod is, as they say in the movies, 'based on a true story'. In 1642, Charles I tried to arrest five MPs, and had the doors of Parliament closed on him.

Black Rod gets paid £101,000 a year, which works out at around £33,600 per strike of his rod. Mind you, that's not all he does: he is also in charge of security in the House of Lords. His opposite number, the Sergeant at Arms, does the same for the House of Commons. In late 2004, however, Parliament felt under siege from terrorists/countryside campaigners/militant fathers etc, so it was suggested that Black Rod and the Sarge hand over the security side of their jobs to professionals. Goodbye Men in Tights, hello Men in Blue.

C IS FOR COLLEGE

… which is the name given to the American voting system. Like us, they don't necessarily reward the party that gets the highest number of votes. It's a bit weird.

It works like this. There are 50 states (51, in effect: but the 51st, Washington, is technically a 'district' and not a state) and each one is allocated a certain number of 'electors'. These electors are absolutely crucial. There are 538 in all. The bigger the state, the more electors they get. California, for example, has 55. Wyoming, on the other hand, has just 3.

The presidential candidate with the most votes in any particular state gets the *entire* allocation of electors put in their column. He (or she, theoretically, although it hasn't happened… yet), for example, might win California by just one vote, but he'll get all 55 of the college votes. And his opponent will get diddly squat. The first one to 270 is the winner.

C IS ALSO FOR COMMITTEES

If it wasn't for these, no laws would ever get passed. For something to become law, it has to go through various committees. And boy, does that take time. Getting an Act on the statute books, like an elephant's pregnancy, can take years and be just as painful.

Before an Act is passed, it's known as a Bill. Often, proposals for a Bill will be contained in something called a White Paper. There are also Green Papers, which are baby versions of White Papers, in that they are, effectively, exercises in kite flying. A White Paper means they're really serious. The current government wants to introduce more 'draft Bills', which are quite exciting, as they get put on the web, so we can all make suggestions. This is what happened in May 2002, with what eventually became the Communications Act.

Bills can be introduced in the Commons or the Lords, but if they're likely to be controversial, they usually start in the Commons. I've listed the procedure below. You never know, it might come in useful some time.

The First Reading is is a bit of a misnomer, as it involves no reading whatsoever. It's just a formality, involving its presentation to the House. It then gets printed.

The Second Reading, which normally occurs within two weeks of the first, is when the general principles of the Bill can be discussed. A gentle tasting session.

The Committee Stage is when the Bill gets a detailed, clause-by-clause examination. Usually, the committee that reads through it (a Standing Committee, as it's known), will have between 16 and 50 members. Politically, it will reflect the make-up of the House of Commons. At this stage, amendments can be suggested, and voted on. Sometimes, if a Bill is really important (eg it's about a treaty enabling us to join the EU) the committee consists of 659 members – ie the entire House of Commons.

The Report Stage is when the Standing Committee reports its amendments etc. back to the House of Commons. This gives MPs who aren't on the committee their chance to stir the pot.

The Third Reading usually comes just seconds, literally, after the Report Stage. This is the final furlong. Big changes cannot now be made. Then, the Bill gets its...

Passage Through To The Other House – ie if it started in the Commons, the Bill goes to the Lords, and vice versa. And what's just happened above, happens all over again. If the second house to look at a Bill wants to change it, the first house has to agree. This can happen several times: some Bills have been known to fly back and forth over the democratic net like a shuttlecock in a game of badminton. However, there are limits on the powers of the Lords – which, if you've been paying attention (see Chapter Six), you'll already know.

The Royal Assent comes when the Bill has completed all its parliamentary stages. It's not actually given by the Queen in person, though. It's just the name given to this last bit. This is when Parliament says, in effect, 'You are a Bill no longer: you are now an Act, my son, and a fully fledged law of the land. Go forth into the world and be free.' The last monarch to refuse the Royal Assent was Queen Anne, in 1707, over a Bill that sought to base the Army in Scotland.

If a Bill doesn't get through a session of Parliament in time – ie it's only reached its Report Stage by the time MPs go off on their hols – then it can be 'carried over' until the next session.

C IS ALSO FOR CONGRESS

This is the American version of our Houses of Parliament. Like ours, it has two bits. Or, if you prefer, it is 'bicameral'. The two halves of Congress are the Senate and the House of Representatives. The Senate has 100 members: 2 for each of the 50 states in America. The House of Representatives – often, and rather confusingly, referred to simply as 'the House' – has 435 people in it. Each state in America gets to send a number of representatives to the House, depending on the size of its population.

The two halves of Congress are generally thought to be equal. However, the House is assumed to be more powerful in financial matters; in foreign affairs, the Senate holds the upper hand.

One of the biggest differences between their system and ours is that their congressional committees, as they're known, are awesomely powerful. The President of the USA may be the mightiest man in the free world, but everything he does, every decision he takes, has to be approved by these committees. And they hate being thought of as a rubber stamp. Congress can be, and often is, one gigantic obstacle. In the UK, we vote on important proposals out in the open, in the House of Commons. Over there, big decisions on new legislation are taken in congressional committees. Not for nothing have they been described as the powerhouses of the American system.

Another big difference is that their system isn't totally dominated by the two big parties, like ours is. Yes, they have two big ones – the Democrats and the Republicans – but a politician's primary loyalty is often to the people, ie the ones that voted for him, rather than his party.

D IS FOR D-NOTICES

These are orders issued by the government that can stop the press printing a story, on the grounds of national security. Let's say a paper got hold of a document revealing the names, locations, duties and tactics of the top ten Britons engaged in the fight against terrorism. The government could slap a D-notice on the paper and it wouldn't be allowed to print it. Mind you, most editors wouldn't even think about running that kind of story in the first place, for obvious reasons.

Helpfully, the government has provided a long list of stories that will attract D-notices, which editors can consult in advance to avoid any nasty accidents. Forbidden stories include any that reveal military plans, operations and capabilities or the whereabouts of nuclear weapons and so-called 'secretive installations'.

The D-notice system was invented in 1912. In 1993 the name was changed to 'DA-notice', but people seem to prefer the old term.

D IS ALSO FOR DEVOLUTION

This is when an upper level of government gives power to a lower one – for instance, when Westminster let Wales, Scotland and Northern Ireland have their own parliaments or assemblies in 1998 and 1999. However, it is important to remember that the upper level of government still holds constitutional power over the lower one, which means the upper one can revoke, or suspend, the lower one's power if it wants to. This is currently the case with Northern Ireland, but it might not be for much longer.

Devolution should not be confused with the F word: 'Federalism'. This is similar, but different. Federalism is where each tier of government has rigid, constitutionally protected areas of power.

E IS FOR ELECTORAL COMMISSION

... which was set up in 2000, to look after all things to do with elections. Among other things, it:

1. Sniffs around the financial affairs of political parties to make sure they're obeying the rules about donations, how much they can spend on their election campaigns, etc.
2. Tries to get more people to vote.

3. Keeps an eye on electoral boundaries. If it found, for example, that one constituency had only 10,000 voters and one MP representing it, but the one next door had 100,000 and also one MP, then it would redraw the boundaries to make things fairer.

F IS FOR FABIAN

This is the name of a society founded in 1884 which was, and still is, dedicated to coming up with well-thought-out ideas on social issues. Fabians don't care much for rampant capitalism; they like the idea of a society based on fairness, brought about by plenty of taxes. They aren't named after Fabian, a moderately successful American rock star of the late 1950s, but Fabius Cunctator. He was a Roman general who used cunning, carefully considered tactics to defeat his arch rival, Hannibal.

Fabians affiliated themselves to the Labour Party after WWI. The playwright George Bernard Shaw was a prominent early Fabian. Nowadays they come out with lots of carefully researched papers on subjects such as reforming the social security system, and whether there should be compulsory voting. (They're broadly in favour.)

F IS FOR FILIBUSTERING

… which is the process of waffling for as long as possible, to kill off a Bill that's being debated in Parliament. It happens in the American Senate a lot more than it does here. That's because new rules were introduced for our Parliament a few years ago, making filibustering more difficult.

The British record for filibustering is held by John Golding, who, in 1983, droned on for more than 11 hours during an all-night sitting at the committee stage of the British Telecommunications Bill. He was trying to stop BT being privatised. (I wouldn't fancy his phone bill.) It worked, in the short term: the Bill didn't become law during that session of Parliament.

G IS FOR GDP

... which stands for Gross Domestic Product. It shows how well, or badly, our economy is doing. GDP is defined as the total value of all goods and services produced in Britain. Even though it has the word 'domestic' in the title, it includes profits earned by foreign firms operating in the UK.

GDP is not to be confused with GNP, which stands for Gross National Product, and takes into account imports and exports. But then again, as any anorak knows, the figure for GNP is nearly always pretty much the same as that for GDP. People used to talk about GNP a lot, but they don't any more: GDP is the term they all use.

G IS ALSO FOR GLOBALISATION

I used to hear this word all the time and never had a clue what it involved. Comfortingly, I'm not alone. Even though countless books and articles have been written about it, no one can agree on a simple definition. But that shouldn't stop you bandying the word about at parties. In fact, I highly recommend it, as it's one of the political buzz words of the early-21st century.

Globalisation is a term that was first used in the late-1960s to describe (takes deep breath, here we go) the fundamental way the world was changing. The boffins realised that individual countries were having their traditional roles, and power, undermined. Suddenly it wasn't all about borders, and us and them; it was more about us. The world as a whole. (I'm generalising a lot here, but globalisation is as general a term as it gets.) This was due to:

1. The massive expansion of international trade and investment.
2. The increased awareness that our actions could have an effect on the world, ie ecologically. Global warming, for example.
3. The increased power of organisations, as opposed to countries – eg multinational businesses/terrorist groups/religious organisations.

Nowadays, globalisation describes all the different processes going on that cut across mere states and societies. We're talking trade, communications and politics: it's not about individual countries, it's about blocks of them, such as the EU and the World Trade Organisation (WTO).

The *effect* of globalisation is what's interesting, though. It's making the world look more and more the same, boffins reckon. Because big multinational businesses bring so many good things with them – such as jobs, wealth, regeneration of local areas etc. – countries all over the world, it's argued, have adopted broadly similar economic policies to attract them. That means not too much government intervention and relatively low taxes on businesses. Is this a good thing or a bad thing? Depends on whether you love or loathe Gap, I guess.

Deep political thinkers have spent years having arguments over globalisation: not just about whether it's good or not, but also, amusingly, about whether it actually *exists*. Sceptics say globalisation is just a figment of some overly intellectual imaginations. Individual states, they argue, are every bit as powerful as they ever were, if not more – just look at the USA.

Globalisation may, then, be just an airy-fairy concept. But it's a very useful one for some people. Especially professors of politics (it gives them something to lecture on), would-be politicians (it gives them something to talk about) and pointy-headed journalists (it gives them something to write about).

G IS ALSO FOR GUEVARA

As in Ernesto 'Che' Guevara, one of the most famous and romanticised political revolutionaries of all time. His most famous image – beret, straggly beard, proud and dignified gaze – has been famous the world over for more than fifty years. He was an Argentinian medical student who had a bit of a road-to-Damascus conversion when he took a motorcycle trip round South America and saw lots of poverty and injustice. He was also a very hardline socialist. So hardline, in fact, that his catchphrase was 'Socialism or death'. He achieved the first part in Cuba in 1959, when he and his mate Fidel Castro launched a successful revolution despite, at one stage, being down to a gang of less than 15 hiding in the mountains. Unfortunately, the second part of his catchphrase occured in 1967: Cuban socialism wasn't hardcore enough for him, so he tried to start another revolution in Bolivia, but was caught and executed.

Che pretty much invented the concept of guerrilla warfare. He wrote a book about it. His theory was that whole armies could be defeated by cunning bands of revolutionaries, provided they realised there was no need to obey the law. The two basic rules of rules of guerrilla warfare, according to Che, were that 1) armed struggle should only take place in the countryside and 2) the city should be where all the cunning, clandestine activity gets carried out.

H IS FOR HOSPITALS (AS IN 'FOUNDATION HOSPITALS')

These are one of New Labour's bright ideas. In 2004 there were about 30 dotted around the country. They could be called 'hermaphrodite hospitals' (but for some reason aren't), as they are a bit of both: part public, part private. Foundation hospitals are run using tax payers' money but differ from NHS hospitals in that they have more control over their own affairs. They don't have to keep answering to the Department of Health all the time, they are inspected less often than NHS places and – most important of all – they can be financially creative with their money. They can borrow cash from banks to build things. They can sell their land and keep the proceeds – as long as they plough it back into 'the business', ie hospital services. They can also pay their staff as much as they like, ignoring national agreements.

This 'not for profit' approach was nicked from the USA and Europe. But it's not popular with everyone and it's too early to say whether it works. Although fans of foundation hospitals say they are efficient, dynamic and responsive, critics say they're unfair. The worry is that they will nick all the best people and have all the best equipment. This could mean – to use a phrase that's always worth trotting out, just to show you know what you're talking about – 'a two-tier health service' (ie foundation hospitals: good. NHS hospitals: not nearly as good).

I IS FOR INDEX (AS IN 'CONSUMER PRICE INDEX')

This is an index that measures changes in the cost of living. It is also one of the Government's favourite ways of measuring inflation, and is interesting only in that it's been subjected to a bit of CGS (Classic Government Sneakiness).

The Consumer Price Index for August 2004, for example, showed an increase of 1.4 per cent compared to the previous year. This was – apparently – mighty impressive, as it suggested that inflation was tightly under control. But according to the economics editor of *The Times*, the cost of living for householders had *actually* increased by 13 per cent during this time. So where did the figure of 1.4 per cent come from? Simple. The Treasury had used a large dollop of CGS when working out the final figure. They had conveniently ignored factors that would have made it bigger – such as the steep rise in house prices and mortgages. That meant they could trumpet a headline figure for inflation that was, arguably, ten times lower than it should have been.

This makes people feel good about the economy. And optimism is very important. But it's also self-delusional and potentially problematic, as it can make people think everything's all right, when it isn't. A bit like a fat man congratulating himself on being able to buy a pair of trousers with a label that reads 'Waist: 34"' when the true size is, in fact, 42".

I IS FOR INSULTS

There is a long list of things you can't call someone in Parliament – such as: 'git', 'hooligan', 'rat', 'swine', 'stoolpigeon', 'jackass', 'nosey parker', 'traitor', 'guttersnipe' and 'murderer'. If an MP uses any of these, they're likely to be ticked off by the Speaker of the House, who is in charge of proceedings, for using 'unparliamentary language'.

Anything that is said in Parliament should be characterised by 'good temper and moderation'. This phrase comes from Erskine May, the book that governs behaviour in the Houses of Parliament. Its full title is actually *Treatise upon the Law, Privileges, Proceedings and Usage of Parliament* and it was written, by the person whose name it bears, in 1844. It's been updated several times since and is also used by other countries whose systems are based on ours.

The worst thing you can call someone in Parliament is 'liar'. However, there are ways to get round this, without getting a yellow card from the Speaker. Winston Churchill, for example, got his message across perfectly by accusing someone of using a 'terminological inexactitude'.

I IS FOR INTERVIEWING

... politicians on the TV and radio. There are two kinds of political interviewer: the smash-them-in-the-face-with-an-iron-fist school (John Humphrys, Jeremy Paxman) and the tap-them-on-the-cheeks-with-a-velvet-glove types (David Frost, Michael Parkinson).

Depending on who you talk to, the Humphrys/Paxo approach is either the best thing to happen to democracy since the Greeks invented it, or a frustrating pantomime that generates more heat than light. One thing you can say, though, is that Paxo asking the then-Home Secretary Michael Howard the same question 14 times ('Did you threaten to overrule him ?') makes for good TV. Whether it *achieves* anything, however, is a different matter. During a programme celebrating *Newsnight*'s anniversary, Paxo asked politicians whether they thought the show had 'changed anything'. They diplomatically changed the subject and the poor bloke looked well disappointed.

The effectiveness of the Frost/Parky style also depends on what you're after. If it's a gas-mark-12 grilling on detailed policy issues you want, forget it. But if you fancy an insight into a politician's character', which is what ticks an awful lot of voters' boxes (and ballot papers), then the Bus Pass Boys are the ones for you.

J IS FOR JERRYMANDERING

Which is usually spelled with a 'G'. But I couldn't think of anything else beginning with a 'J' for this entry, so Jerrymandering it is. This is the sneaky practice of redrawing the boundaries of electoral districts so you get an unfair advantage next time there's a vote. In crude terms, it would mean cutting out an area where you know lots of people wouldn't vote for you, but including a district where you are guaranteed lots of support.

The word was coined in 1812, after the Governor of Massachusetts, Elbridge Gerry, approved a brand new district which, on paper, looked like a salamander.

('Gerry' and 'salamander' – geddit?) Anyway, it worked: Gerry's party won a majority of the seats on offer.

There are three basic tactics involved in gerry-mandering, catchily known as 'stacking', 'packing' and 'cracking'. 'Stacking' is when you redraw a boundary so that your opponents are in a minority. 'Packing' is when you make sure that your opponents are packed into a small number of constituencies. And 'cracking' is when you divide your opponents between a large number of constituencies.

Trivia time: one of the most famous recent examples of gerrymandering/jerrymandering involved the Tory party's Dame Shirley Porter, who led Westminster City Council in the late 1980s. She hatched a plot to boost votes by selling off cut price council houses to potential Tory supporters. Dame Shirley is the daughter of Sir Jack Cohen, who built up Tesco. He came up with the name 'Tesco' by combining the first syllable of the names of Dame Shirley's mum, TESsa COhen. Just like they did with GERRY and salaMANDER. Spooky coincidence or what! (I thought it was interesting, anyway.)

K IS FOR KEYNSIAN

You can't talk about the economy in an intelligent way (or pretend to, at any rate) without mentioning John Maynard Keynes. He gave his name to a type of economic policy that was hugely influential for long periods after WWII. It involved the government taking the economic bull by the horns, intervening a lot, and spending loads, in order to create lots of jobs. Keynsian economic policy was very popular until the mid-1970s, but then we got into an economic crisis and the rival school of thinking – 'Monetarism' – became more fashionable. (See below.) The problem with Keynes was that his theories weren't big on tackling inflation. If you're desperate to know more you could always attempt to wade your way through Keynes's exciting 1936 masterpiece – curiously featuring neither sex scenes nor car chases – called *The General Theory of Employment, Interest and Money*.

If you come over all previous and unnecessary when the subject turns to economics, don't worry, you're in good company. Sir Alec Douglas-Home, who was PM from 1963 to 1964, once said: 'There are two problems in my life. The political ones are insoluble and the economic ones are incomprehensible.'

L IS FOR LOTHIAN (AS IN 'THE WEST LOTHIAN QUESTION')

… which is all about the influence that English MPs have over Scotland, and vice versa. The question was originally asked by Labour MP Tam Dalyell, who used to represent the Scottish constituency of West Lothian, and basically it is this:

How can it be right that Scottish MPs at Westminster can vote on English matters, while MPs from England have lost the power to influence Scottish affairs, as they are now controlled by the Scottish Parliament in Edinburgh?

There are several possible answers to this question:

1. That's life, pal. It might sound unfair, but then so was the fact that Scotland spent most of the 1980s and 1990s voting Labour, only to end up getting ruled, throughout that period, by the Tories.

2. Westminster voted to give Scotland its own parliament, so it was actually responsible for creating this situation in the first place. It's no use MPs in Westminster complaining about it now.

3. You could always reduce the number of Scottish MPs at Westminster. At the moment, there are 72. Noises have been made about cutting that down to 58, but it hasn't happened yet.

4. You could always split the House of Commons up, and give England its own parliament.

5. Scottish MPs could always do the honourable thing and choose to absent themselves from matters of a purely English nature.

At the moment, the West Lothian Question isn't being asked very often. But if the Tories got in again, it might. Especially if they only had a small majority: the inconvenience of seventy-odd Scottish Labour MPs voting against them all the time would be considerable.

M IS FOR MONETARISM

In the 1960s, you were a fan of either the Beatles or the Stones. But if you wore glasses, didn't go out much and preferred reading books on economics, you were either Monetarist or Keynsian. Modern Monetarism was invented by an American economist Milton Friedman and his chums from the so-called 'Chicago School' of thinking. And Mrs Thatcher, for one, was *very* much in their camp.

Monetarists are obsessed with low inflation: they think it's more important than anything else, even keeping everyone in work. Monetarists say the best way to keep inflation low is to tightly control the money supply, ie the amount of money in circulation. If you want to know what happens when you print too much money, they say, look at Germany in 1923. They printed loads, to try and get out of an economic crisis. But the more notes they printed, the more inflation there was. Soon it was running at several million per cent. It got to the stage where the notes weren't worth the paper they were printed on, and you needed a wheelbarrow full just to buy a frankfurter.

N IS FOR NATO

… which stands for North Atlantic Treaty Organisation. This was a group of 19 countries – all European, apart from the USA and Canada – which came together on 4 April 1949 to counter the power of the Soviet bloc and the so-called 'Reds under the bed' (ie Soviet infiltrators in the West). Its purpose, as one wag put it nice and succinctly, was to: 'Keep the Americans in, the Germans down and the Russians out.'

It's still going, even though the threat of communist expansion has long since passed. Which is why many commentators now accuse NATO of being as useful, and relevant, as a shop selling sand in the Sahara – especially now that the European Union is starting to think about how to defend itself. But NATO was called on a lot during the Balkan crisis of the mid-1990s, and to disband it now would be to waste more than fifty years of military cooperation and planning. The thinking seems to be this: it ain't completely broke, so why ditch it?

For the record, here are the current members: Belgium, Bulgaria, Canada, the Czech Republic, Denmark, Estonia, France, Germany, Greece, Hungary, Iceland, Italy, Latvia, Lithuania, Luxembourg, the Netherlands, Norway, Poland, Portugal, Romania, Slovakia, Slovenia, Spain, Turkey, the UK and the USA.

O IS FOR OECD

... which stands for the Organisation for Economic Cooperation and Development. A massive talking shop based in Paris, it employs 2,400 people and churns out endless reports and lots of economic data. There are 30 countries in the OECD, including most of Europe, Australia, the USA and Canada. It has lots of worthy aims, such as making the environment better and helping poorer countries get richer. It hasn't actually achieved a huge amount, however, apart from the destruction of several thousand trees.

P IS FOR PFI

Not to be confused with MFI, which sells cheap furniture. There is nothing remotely cheap about PFI: we're talking billions here. PFI stands for Private Finance Initiative. It's another New Labour Big Idea, but one that was actually invented by the Tories.

This is how it works. You are the government. You want lots of new schools/hospitals/prisons/roads. But you don't want to pay for them by raising income taxes, as that's a bit of a vote loser. So you get a private company to build the school/hospital/prison/road instead. And you then make large, regular payments to that company over a period of 25 to 30 years. You also get a private company to run it for you.

New Labour have been doing a lot of these deals: £100 billion has been set aside to spend on PFI projects over the next 30 years. They think it's a good idea, as private companies are less likely to overspend and be inefficient, given that it's their money which is at risk. The figures suggest this might be true. In 2003, a National Audit Office report looked into more than 550 PFI projects. Seventy-five per cent were delivered on time, and 100 per cent came in bang on budget. Previously, when it was public money involved, only 30 per cent came in on time, and just 27 per cent on budget.

But some people hate the PFI. They say it's creative accounting, as it makes the nation's balance sheet look healthier than it really is. This is because it takes so many hugely expensive items out of the equation. And, they argue, there's no real risk involved for the private companies taking part, as if it all goes pear-shaped, they know that the government will always bail them out.

P IS ALSO FOR POLITICAL PROGRAMMES ON TV

... which, in the main, are as dull as ditchwater and watched by the TV equivalent of one man and his dog. The BBC was so worried by this that it spent tens of thousands of pounds on a study into how to make its political programmes better. As a result they ditched a Sunday lunchtime show featuring an old bloke in a suit interviewing a politician in a suit for an hour and replaced it with a Sunday lunchtime show where a middle-aged bloke in a suit interviews a politician in a suit for an hour.

Some good did come out of it, however: *Weekend with Rod Liddle*, which went out at 9am on a Saturday morning on BBC2. It featured a fat, middle-aged presenter trying to ingratiate himself with a young audience and was glorious, ankle-chewing, granddad-down-the-disco stuff. Despite the best efforts of the BBC to keep it hidden away, the critics found it. One Sunday newspaper described it as one of the worst programmes ever seen on British TV. Others put it in the SOBIB category: So Bad, It's Brilliant. Unfortunately, the BBC took it off after just three episodes. Not all political programmes are duds, however: BBC1's *Question Time* does very well in the ratings, despite not having changed its format in over 25 years and is still a consistently good watch.

Question Time aside, it's mightily difficult to do a political show that is fresh, credible and entertaining, but also pulls in the viewers. *Newsnight*, for example, regularly gets less than a million viewers and is regarded as an irrelevance by politicians. That hasn't stopped people trying, though. ITV1 are due to do a show in January 2005 called *Vote for Me*. It's Popstars meets politics, basically. Lots of ordinary people who fancy being MPs will be put through a series of tests by a panel of expert judges. A public vote decides the winner. Already, however, Alistair Campbell has slagged it off – without seeing it – calling it 'another crap reality show.' I hope he's wrong: I'm presenting it.

The issue of political programmes on TV is an important one – but only for two groups of people. Politicians – because they want to see more of themselves on TV. And broadcasters – because they need to keep in with the politicians. No one else gives a toss.

P IS FOR POLITICS

We use the word all the time. But what does it mean? *The Concise Oxford Dictionary of Politics* (by Iain McLean and Alistair McMillan – very academic, as much fun as food poisoning, but useful) defines it as 'the practice of the art and science of administrating states'. For the rest of us – the non boffins – it's pretty much anything that involves people who call themselves 'politicians'. In other words, politics = what is said, or done by, politicians.

But this is a bit of a narrow definition. Interestingly, lots of very brainy people have had very long arguments over what is and isn't politics. The feminist brigade, for example (a lot of whom live in Stoke Newington, north London) argue that all the personal stuff in our lives is, essentially, political: all aspects of the relationship between a man and a woman, for instance.

Others go even further. They claim that everything we do or say, no matter how seemingly trivial, has a political implication. Take going to the bog. Hard paper? Soft? Recyclable? That's a highly political decision if you think about it. The Amazonian rainforests could ultimately be at stake. (Something to think about next time you're sitting there. In fact, maybe you are, right now.)

Arguably, then, politics is much *more* than what politicians come up with: it's about how all of us conduct our lives, and how we try to make ourselves happy. Curiously and distressingly, however, the mighty Sir David Dimbleby (it's only a matter of time) appears to disagree. He clearly thinks politics is nothing to do with the pursuit of happiness. Once, during an episode of *Question Time* just before a general election, an audience member stood up and asked, 'Which party will make us happiest?' Sir Dave, deciding the question wasn't even worth an answer, did his 'Yes, right, anyone else? You, in the red shirt' bit and moved swiftly on. This was a rare mistake, I feel. The question 'Which party will make us happiest' is, arguably, the most incisive and relevant political question it's possible to ask. Why do you think governments try to cut NHS waiting lists and improve our schools? That's right. To make us happy.

But as we all know, the word 'politics' has a bad reputation. People associate it with irrelevance, boredom and a lack of trust. A shame: now that I'm finishing this book, I've realised that it's genuinely, endlessly, fascinating. Fathers 4 Justice, fox hunting, what we see on TV, sport, sex – it's all politics. If you're bored with politics, you're bored with life.

Q IS FOR AL-QAIDA

… which, translated, means 'The Base'. It's led by Osama bin Laden, who is a lot more wealthy than you might have realised, which is very important if you're trying to fund the world's premier global terror network. It's claimed, although this has been heavily disputed, that his inherited fortune is around $300 million. He is also said to own, via a complex system of trusts and the like, a range of businesses around the world. They include banks, farms and factories. He also gets a lot of financial support from some Islamic charities and organisations, although the FBI are doing their best to stop that: since 2001, it's said they've frozen around $125 million of Laden's assets.

Bin Laden wasn't always rabidly anti-American, though: he started off hating the Soviets and fought against them when they occupied Afghanistan in the mid-1980s. But when they withdrew, he went to live in Saudi Arabia, where he'd been brought up. It was there that he found his new enemy. During the 1991 Gulf War, he developed a profound loathing of the United States. He could not abide the fact that Western troops were based in his country, a holy place. It was, for him, a violation.

He also despised Israel and didn't think it had the right to even exist. Another reason to hate the Americans, who appeared to be strongly pro-Israeli.

Bin Laden made his way back to Afghanistan in the late 1990s and began planning a series of attacks. They started with the bombing of American embassies in Kenya and Tanzania, and culminated in the events of 11 September 2001, when planes hijacked by al-Qaida devotees were deliberately flown into the Pentagon building in Washington DC and the twin towers of the World Trade Centre in New York. More than 3,000 people were killed.

'Operation Enduring Freedom' was supposed to destroy bin Laden, and al-Qaida, but it's unclear how successful it's been in either of these aims. Have bin Laden and his organisation been fatally wounded, or just temporarily disrupted?

R IS FOR REPUBLICANS AND DEMOCRATS: WHAT'S THE DIFFERENCE?

These are the two main parties in the United States. In the old days, the Republicans were a bit like our

Tories, and the Democrats were the equivalent of Labour. But now that the Labour Party has stolen most of the Tories' clothes, that comparison doesn't really work any more.

Put simply, the Republican Party (also known as the GOP: the Grand Old Party) favours business and opposes welfare. The Democrats, on the other hand, are traditionally said to be keen on welfare, minority interests and big government, ie, one that employs loads of people and gets involved in lots of different areas in its citizens' lives. Republicans usually have a stronger, or more 'hawkish' foreign policy than Democrats.

But the important thing to remember is that the party system over there is much weaker and far more open than ours. In most states in the USA, you can suddenly decide that you're a Democrat – or a Republican – and run for office using that label. In Britain, you can't do that.

R IS FOR RULE (AS IN THE 'TEN-MINUTE RULE')

You are an MP. You think an issue is so important it needs to be aired in the House of Commons and therefore brought to the attention of the public and the press. There are lots of ways of doing this, and the Ten-Minute Rule is one of them. It gives an MP the right to speak, briefly, about something that they think is important. Another MP then speaks, equally briefly, against the proposal. However, parliamentary rules state that this can only happen on Tuesdays and Wednesdays.

Others ways for MPs to get it off their chests in the Commons, without the hassle of trying to get legislation on the books, include:

Question Time. This is a chance to put a minister on the spot. Ministers answer questions on a rota basis and there's a lot of competition to ask them something. Success depends on 'catching the Speaker's eye', ie getting him or her to give you permission to speak.

Adjournment Debates. These usually last half an hour and are the last business of the day. They are much sought after, and your best chance of getting one is to be chosen by ballot. If you're lucky, though, the Speaker will give you your own debate, without your needing to enter the prize draw.

Early Day Motions (EDMs). Nothing to do with All Bran, but a way of placing on the record an MP's opinion about a subject. EDMs usually aren't debated in the House, but are useful ways of seeing whether an issue has any 'legs'.

S IS FOR SUBSIDIARITY

… which happens when power ebbs away from those on high, to those down below. The term has been used most often in relation to the EU. In that context, it describes a situation in which the member states have more control over their own affairs than cumbersome institutions at the top, such as the European Parliament. When John Major was PM, politicians everywhere got very hot under the collar about subsidiarity. But then they realised that:

1. No one gave a toss.

2. No one knew what they were talking about. And…

3. … neither, if truth be told, did they.

As a result, the word is hardly ever used now.

T IS FOR THINK TANKS

… which are organisations that spend all day thinking up interesting, exciting new policy ideas and solutions to problems that haven't even happened yet. Some have Greek-sounding names, such as Civitas, Politeia and Demos, while others favour the more impressive-sounding 'Centre' or 'Institute' tag, ie 'The Centre for Policy Studies' and 'The Institute for Public Policy Research'. There are so many of them that there is even a 'Think Tank of the Year' award.

If a think tank is lucky, its reports will be read by, and maybe even influence, someone important in government. This is what happened with the Centre for Policy Studies. In the 1970s, it came up with lots of ideas for creating wealth, and getting rid of cumbersome, annoying regulations. A lot of its ideas were then put into practice by Mrs Thatcher.

In theory, think tanks are a very good idea, as governments are too busy governing to think effectively about problems that haven't yet occurred. However, there are problems with think tanks. Money is one: there aren't too many people prepared to finance people just to think. Think tanks also have more competition now: universities and pressure groups come up with a lot of 'blue sky thinking' these days. Finally, a lot of bright young things who work for think tanks leave, not surprisingly, to join governments, where they can put their ideas into practice, rather than onto paper.

U IS FOR UNITED NATIONS

In 1958, 13 years after this organisation came into being, Eddie Cochran sang of taking his problem to 'the Yew-nited Nations'. But he didn't. This may have been because his problem − the 'Summertime Blues' − wasn't covered by the UN's charter. The organisation was, and still is, more concerned with preserving world peace and solving economic, social and political problems throughout the world. It is also big on promoting human rights: but not on curing the Summertime Blues.

When it started, it had 51 countries. Now it has 189 and nearly every nation in the world is a member. The UN's headquarters are in New York. The organisation is going through a bit of a crisis at the moment, as it failed to agree a second resolution that would have given the official green light for the 2002 invasion of Iraq. Critics say it has therefore failed to live up to the challenges of the 21st century, and that it's now in huge danger of becoming redundant and irrelevant.

But defenders say it's the best − and indeed, only − body we have that acts as a keeper of world peace. Life without it, they say, would be very scary indeed, as

261

countries such as the USA, and others, could simply do whatever they wanted, without permission or agreement from anyone. Cynics, of course, would say that's exactly what America does anyway.

V IS FOR VIRTUAL REPRESENTATION

… which has nothing to do with computers but a lot to do with people who thought giving the vote to poor people/women/the young was a bad idea. 'They don't need the ability to vote,' so the argument went, 'because they have virtual representation. We know what they need, what they want, and what's best for them. Giving them the vote would muck things up.'

This didn't wash, obviously, as it was patronising and undemocratic. But there's actually nothing wrong with the concept itself, which is still in evidence today: children, for example, are virtually represented.

W IS FOR WIDDECOMBE RULES

But not as in 'Ann Widdecombe Rules OK'. Quite the opposite, in fact. In the 1980s, Ann Widdecombe, who was then a Tory minister, decreed that if you had a good job in local government, you couldn't be a local councillor or MP. As a result, any council employee earning over £32,127 cannot now stand for election.

Many think the so-called 'Widdecombe Rules' are bonkers: it's not as if millions of us are queuing up to stand for election, so why rule out so many highly qualified people ?

Someone with a good job in local government, it's argued, is *just* the sort of person we should be encouraging. Barring them from standing is like banning professional soccer players from being football managers. An organisation called the Local Government Information Unit is currently campaigning to have the Widdecombe Rules abolished.

W IS ALSO FOR WRITTEN CONSTITUTION

The UK doesn't have one. Should it? This is an important question. But one that can be heroically dull. It makes even politicians dream of duvets. The Conservative Party, for example, showed their attitude to the subject when they simply axed the post of Party Spokesman for Constitutional Affairs altogether.

Interestingly, we are a democratic sore thumb in this respect. There are only two democracies in the world who don't have a written constitution. Us and Israel. Draw your own conclusions.

Our constitution is actually codified. That is, it's a bit higgledy-piggledy. There are several sources of it: some are written down, some aren't. The written bits include Acts of Parliament, European Union Law, treaties and the odd highly respected constitutional bestseller – and you don't get many of those to the pound – like Walter Bagehot's 1867 blockbuster, *The English Constitution*.

The unwritten bits are called 'conventions' and 'common law': these are customs that are so old, and have been followed so rigidly, that they have the force of law. The royal prerogative, for example, comes under this heading. There's no written law saying what it is, or isn't. We just, kind of, *know*.

There are those who argue that the whole thing should be written down, in what would basically be a fully binding national rule book. To make it stick, there would need to be new rules and a stipulation that the constitution could only be altered if at least two-thirds of *both* Houses of Parliament agreed.

People who support a written constitution say it would be a great idea, as it would make things much clearer, ie turn grey areas into black-and-white ones. It would make the courts a bit stronger, compared to Parliament: at the moment, it's argued, the latter can trample far too easily over decisions made by the former.

And it would also protect us if mad nutter extremists ever got into power and wanted to disregard democratic procedures. Then we could simply turn around and say to them: 'You can't do that, it's not in the constitution.'

Opponents, however, say we don't need one. If it ain't broke, don't fix it. And the public aren't exactly clamouring for it either, so why bother? What's more, it's a bit undemocratic – because the people who would ultimately decide on important constitutional matters would be judges, and they're unelected. Out-of-touch coffin-dodgers, even. It's also highly inflexible, they say. If we made hard-and-fast rules, which were massively difficult to change, we could be storing up problems for ourselves. We might know what's best for us now, but what about in a hundred years' time? Finally, they point out, countries with written constitutions aren't always shiny, happy beacons of democracy. They might have a point here. Iraq – under the rule of one S. Hussein esq. – had a written constitution.

X IS FOR 'X-ECUTIVE'

... or, as it is more commonly known, the executive. This is a useful x-cuse to x-plain a very important piece of political thinking that underpins our entire system: the theory of the Separation of Powers. This is the idea that the powers of a sovereign government (such as ours) should be split between two, or more, completely separate parts. This way, no one person or group can gain too much power. (As I said, it's only a theory.)

Our system actually has three parts:

1.) The executive: this is the bit that implements – executes – the law of the land. In our system, the executive is the government: ie the PM, his Cabinet and his MPs.

2.) The judiciary: this is the bit that interprets the law. Otherwise known as the courts.

3.) The legislature: this is the bit that makes the law. In our system, that is Parliament – ie the whole shooting match: the Commons and the Lords.

What is slightly confusing is that the theory is called 'The *Separation* of Powers' and yet the three items listed

265

above are not, actually, separate at all: the executive (the government) is also part of the legislature (Parliament). Nevertheless, so the theory goes, that shouldn't stop the latter keeping an eye on the former, and the judiciary keeping an eye on both.

Z IS FOR ZIONISM

Originally, 'Zionism' was the name given to the movement aimed at giving Jews their own nation – Israel – in what was then Palestine. They got that in 1948. Since then it has generally been used to describe the support given to Jews by the West, particularly in America.

The cause of modern Zionism was initially promoted by Hungarian-born journalist Theodor Herzl, the first person to come to the conclusion that the Jews needed their own homeland. He did so after reporting on the infamous Dreyfus Case in 1894, the story that put anti-Semitism on the 20th-century map. Alfred Dreyfus was a French army officer of Jewish descent who was imprisoned after being accused of treachery. There was an international protest over his treatment – many felt he had been the victim of blatant anti-Semitism – and in 1906 he was finally exonerated and given a full pardon.

In 1917, 23 years after Herzl set the ball rolling, Zionism got a massive and historic fillip: the Balfour Declaration. This was a letter, signed by the then British Foreign Secretary, AJ Balfour, which gave a massive thumbs up to 'a national home for the Jewish people' in

Palestine, provided the rights of the 'existing non-Jewish communities' there would be respected. The communities in question were the Arab Palestinians.

After WWII, and the killing of 6 million Jews by the Nazis, it was only a matter of time before the Jewish people got their national homeland. For one thing, there were hundreds of thousands of Jewish refugees from Europe who felt they had nowhere safe to go. Moreover, there was worldwide sympathy at what had happened to them during the Holocaust – and guilt that more hadn't been done to prevent it.

The state of Israel came into being at midnight on 14 May 1948. And the very next day, Arab armies invaded Israel, kick-starting the first Arab-Israeli war.

The consequences of the creation of the state of Israel are still being felt today, as you may have noticed. The Israeli-Palestinian issue is, arguably, the longest-running and most difficult issue in modern world politics. Despite there being 'a road map' to peace in the Middle East, many involved appear to have either lost their way for the time being, or taken a very long stop-off at a motorway service station. In late 2004 noises were again being made about 'finding a solution.' Maybe this time...

Epilogue

It's a grim, horrible Saturday night and I am in a state of genuine excitement. What has brought this about? Have the mighty Charlton Athletic just dispatched Manchester United 5–0 and qualified for next season's European Champions League? No. Have I just seen my sixth, winning, number come up on the National Lottery? Wrong again. An offer to take over from Parkinson on ITV1 on Saturday nights, perhaps? Regrettably, no.

The reason – and I can't believe I'm saying it, because before this book, it would have been unthinkable – is that I've just come back from a political debate at a theatre in Cheltenham. I'm buzzing, I kid you not. I yapped about it with my wife in the car all the way home. And I don't think I'm the only one feeling like this. Halfway through the event I looked at some of the 1500 faces in the audience (it was a sellout). It was the first time I'd managed to lever my eyes from the stage. Everyone was rapt. They looked spellbound, like they were watching the final scenes of a really good thriller. Remarkable really: on stage were simply three blokes sitting on chairs, discussing politics. No props, no music, no sex, just 90 minutes of non-stop, pure politics. The theme was 'Who Runs Britain?' and taking part were Michael White, the political editor of the Guardian (amusing), Anthony Sampson, who wrote The Anatomy of Britain in the 1960s (well impressive) and Tony Wright, political scientist and new Labour MP (strangely likeable).

They talked about how too much power was vested in the Prime Minister, why we went to war and big business.

The most interesting bit for me was when Anthony Sampson exploded one of the myths about invading Iraq, ie that 'we went to war because of oil'. Helpfully – and unfashionably – Sampson had actually spoken with two very important and relevant people: the British heads of BP and Shell. Both told him they were actually dead against the war, because it might destabilise the region and, eventually, put oil supplies at risk. They may well be proved right.

Anyway, so much for the cliche that people 'just aren't interested in politics'. That, I'm afraid, is bollocks. It may have been the case, a bit, once, but it's not any more. And I'm not just basing that on what I saw in Cheltenham. For a start, films about politics have become the new Westerns. The Yanks seem to be churning out one a month. And there's a massive audience for them. Michael Moore's Farenheit 9/11, about the war in Iraq may, in parts, be comically misleading, but it's also the highest-grossing documentary of all time.

Now look at the turnouts for the two elections held in Spain and America in 2004. Both were unexpectedly massive. In Spain it was 77 per cent. And 120 million Americans voted this time around – that's 20 million more than usual. Ironically, part of the credit (blame?) for this should go to al-Qaida. Their avowed aim may be to smash Western democracy to bits, but instead they seem to have achieved precisely the opposite: given it a ruddy great shot in the arm. I bet you something similar happens in Britain in the general election of 2005. The turnout at the last one was 59 per cent – I bet my house it'll be higher this time. In fact, I'm bunging a hundred quid on it being more than 70 per cent.

Another irony: I've turned into the sort of person I used to avoid at parties. Once, if people started on politics, I'd think 'hello... bores' and pretend I needed the bog. But now I've reached the end of this book, I realise it wasn't they who were boring, it was me. Only the other week I met a small, odd-looking bloke with bulging eyes at a friend's 40th. He started talking about the then-forthcoming American elections. He assured me the Democrats' John Kerry would walk it because, he said, lots more Hispanics, Latinos and black people were going to vote this time around and most of them were Democrats. Anyway, that's not the point, this is: once, I'd have gone into reverse gear the moment he started and sought out the honey and mustard cocktail sausages. But this time I spent half-an-hour with him, chewing a more satisfying kind of fat. I have, I think, become what they call 'highly politicised' – and I like it. I hope you have been, and that you like it, too.

JM
The Shed at the Bottom of the Garden
Chiswick
West London
January 2005
jmaitland@ukgateway.net

Acknowledgements

- Ligia Teixeira for her incredible hard work, commitment, tolerance and enthusiasm.

- James Macintyre for being supportive, creative, ingenious, diligent and having impeccable contacts.

- Dan, James's flatmate, for helping me penetrate the first thickets of the European Union jungle.

- Matthew Parris for generosity, insights and advice well beyond the call of duty.

- John Humphrys, Bob Worcester, Dr Alan Sked, Ben Lucas, Devon Allison, Carole Karp, Jessica Litten, Lord Norton of Louth, Simon Heywood, Derek Draper and Jane West for letting me interview them (or not, in the last case).

- Professor Fred Halliday of the London School of Economics for reading through and advising on the Islamic Bit.

- David Cracknell for his time, advice and opinion.

- Steve Anderson 4 voting 4 me 4 Vote 4 Me.

- Inda 'Inda House' Rana for technical support at all times of day and night, from wherever in the world I happened to be.

- The chimps/aka the housemates/aka Felix and Ivo for being well-behaved and not arguing too violently, too often.

- John Blake for – pardon the Americanism – 'believing in the project' when no one else did.

- Julian Worricker for reading through an early draft and making suggestions.

- David Leach and colleagues at Mentorn TV for not being too obstructive.

- Emily, my wife, for lots of love and support. Sorry for ruining your summer.

- You, for reading this book. But only if you've paid for it.